leading

with

noble
purpose

leading
with **noble**
purpose

How *to* Create
a Tribe *of* True Believers

Lisa Earle McLeod

WILEY

Published by John Wiley & Sons, Inc., Hoboken, New Jersey.
Published simultaneously in Canada.

For general information on our other products and services or for technical support, please contact our Customer Care Department within the United States at (800) 762–2974, outside the United States at (317) 572–3993 or fax (317) 572–4002.

Wiley also publishes its books in a variety of electronic formats. Some content that appears in print may not be available in electronic books. For more information about Wiley products, visit our website at www.wiley.com.

Library of Congress Cataloging-in-Publication Data is available:

978-1-119-11980-7 (hbk)
978-1-119-11983-8 (epdf)
978-1-119-11981-4 (epub)

Cover Design: Wiley
Cover Image: © iStock.com/VikaSuh

Printed in the United States of America

10 9 8 7 6 5 4 3 2 1

Written with love
in honor of
Julius Richard "Jay" Earle, Jr.
August 14, 1936–July 21, 2015
husband, father, leader, and friend

Contents

Introduction:
Why Work
Matters

What if your work mattered so much to you that—on your deathbed—you found yourself wishing for one more day at the office?

While I was writing this book, my father died. In the months before his death, I had time to reminisce with him about his life's high points, among them, his job.

My father worked in banking. At the height of his career he was Director of Mergers and Acquisitions for the Federal Savings and Loan Insurance Corporation, the FSLIC, which later merged into the FDIC. During the S&L crisis of the 1980s he ran a team whose purpose was to merge failing banks with solvent banks, so taxpayers wouldn't have to foot the bill if an S&L went under.

In his office, my father kept a flipchart tracking how much money his department saved the U.S. taxpayers. He updated that chart weekly and shared it with anyone who walked into his office. Financial experts estimated that my father and his team saved the taxpayers *billions* of dollars. The stakes were high. The work was difficult, but his team was passionate about it because they knew it mattered.

We've all heard the adage: No one on their deathbed wishes they'd spent more time at the office. I think that adage is misunderstood. It belittles the role that meaningful work plays in our lives. A 2005 study of terminal cancer patients found that, once the patients finished talking about their families, some of their most meaningful experiences involved doing work that mattered with people they cared about.

That study mirrors what I experienced with my father. My father loved his family. By the standards of the day, he spent significantly more time with his kids than most men. He changed diapers, coached, did home projects, camped. He even learned how to score gymnastics to help my high school team.

But he also loved his job. When my father had fallen ill, reading notes from his former colleagues was a high point for him. He loved talking about the good times, and the bad, the obstacles they'd faced, the deals that had gone well, and the deals that hadn't. My father swelled with pride as he talked about his team and the impact they'd had on the banking system.

It's easy to say family is the most important thing. Yet, watching my father reflect upon his life, it's obvious to me—work matters. We spend most of our waking hours at work, so those hours ought to mean something.

Viktor Frankl once said, "Life is never made unbearable by circumstances, but only by lack of meaning and purpose."

Human beings are hardwired for purpose. Once you get beyond food, shelter, air, and water, human beings have two core needs: connection and meaning. We want to make a difference. We want our lives to count for something. This emotional need transcends sex, race, age, and culture. If we don't satisfy that core need, we die—first emotionally, then physically.

Unfortunately, many people see their work as devoid of higher purpose. Instead, they view it as a grind—as an endless series of meaningless tasks.

A May 2014 op-ed piece in the *New York Times*, "Why You Hate Work,"[1] was the most emailed article for a week. That piece revealed that, in a 2013 Harvard study of white-collar workers, over half failed to feel any connection to the company's mission, nor any level of workplace meaning and significance.

We know the Gallup numbers; lack of employee engagement has reached epidemic proportions. Gallup's latest research reveals that 51 percent of people are not engaged in their work, and an additional 17 percent are actively disengaged.

When I talk about these figures during a speech, I say to the audience, "Look at the person sitting next to you. At least one of you hates your job." It always gets a laugh. They laugh, not because it's funny, but because it's true.

These are more than business statistics. These are real live human beings who spend the majority of their waking hours doing something they don't care about.

It's not work itself that kills our spirit. It's meaningless work. I often hear leaders lamenting that employees "just don't care anymore." Maybe the reason for this employee malaise is that leadership hasn't given them anything meaningful to care about. People want to be part of something bigger than themselves. In fact, they're desperate for it.

Employee engagement is not the root problem. It's a symptom. The real problem is lack of workplace meaning.

How did we get here?

It's simple: We put profit before purpose, and in doing so, eroded the very thing that makes a business great.

We've made some faulty assumptions about work, and those assumptions are killing us. We've allowed the money story to replace the meaning story. The narrative of earnings and bonuses that was

---

[1] Tony Schwartz and Christine Porath, "Why You Hate Work," *New York Times*, May 30, 2014.

supposed to improve employee performance has had the opposite effect. It has stripped the joy and meaning from work in ways that have a chilling effect on morale, performance, service, and ultimately profit itself.

It's time to face reality. Money is not a sustainable motivator. People want money; they also want meaning. Without a higher purpose, your organization is doomed to mediocrity. We live in an age where businesses can exist in the cloud. We've moved from a production economy, to an idea economy. It's been well-documented, purpose drives engagement *and* profit. Consider this:

- A 10-year growth study of 50,000 brands shows that companies who put improving people's lives at the center of all they do have growth rates that are triple that of their competitors, and they outperform the market by 383 percent.[2]
- Deloitte's 2015 workplace survey reveals the tight correlation between purpose and profit. Deloitte chairman Punit Renjen said, "A strong sense of purpose drives businesses to take the long view and invest for growth." Purpose increases customer, employee, and shareholder engagement.
- Our firm, McLeod & More, Inc.'s, field research with over 500 sales organizations revealed that salespeople who sell with Noble Purpose, who truly want to make a difference in the lives of their customers, outsell salespeople focused on targets and quotas.

Ironic isn't it? The way to a more profitable company is to put purpose, rather than profit, at the center.

Traditional wisdom has told us that emotions don't belong at work. This idea isn't just wrong; it's insane.

---

[2]From Jim Stengel's study of business growth, conducted in collaboration with Millward Brown Optimor: a 10-year growth study utilizing Millward Brown Optimor's global database of more than 50,000 brands.

When was the last time you heard a CEO say, "I wish my people weren't so excited"? Have you ever wished that your suppliers were less passionate? Have you ever wanted a customer service person to be a little *less* caring? Have you ever wished that you yourself were less enthusiastic about your own work?

Of course not.

Yet somewhere along the line we allowed ourselves to get derailed. We decided that spreadsheets could produce results, and that profit was enough incentive for everyone. Leaders started to believe that *measuring* money would somehow *produce* money. We tried to ignore emotions in favor of metrics, but money is not produced in a vacuum. It's the output of a multi-faceted human ecosystem. We confused the results with the process. Great organizations are *driven* by qualitative strategies; their success is *measured* by quantitative results. The crisis of disengaged employees only proves what we already know in our hearts to be true. **You can't spreadsheet your way to passion.**

Leading with Noble Purpose aims to rectify this problem. Noble Purpose is a business growth strategy. It's also much more. It's a call for today's leaders to set the bar higher, for themselves, their people, and their organizations. It's about bringing meaning back into the workplace.

Noble Purpose is a strategic shift in the way you approach business. Instead of focusing on internal metrics, a Noble Purpose strategy is built upon the external impact you have on your customers, the real live human beings who benefit from your services. Revenue, profit, and productivity are indicators of how well you're performing against your purpose.

The stakes are high; the pace of work has accelerated, and the pressure is real. There's no denying that. Work is competitive, work is hard, and work can be exhausting. But work should not be soul-suckingly awful.

The current business model is failing us, and it's failing our people. It's time for us to better.

■ ■ ■

A friend of mine who works in politics once told me, "In every office there's always a TB."

"What's a TB?" I asked her.

"A TB," she said, "is a True Believer. They're that starry-eyed optimist who still believes that they can make a difference. But here's the thing all the jaded staffers don't tell you, everyone else is secretly jealous of the TB."

I've come to understand the reason people are jealous of the True Believer is because we all want to feel that level of passion and pride about our own work.

When it came to work, my father was a True Believer. He led a team of people through an industry crisis. They came out on the other side proud of what they had accomplished. My father believed that their work mattered and that being a good boss was a noble calling. He was right.

For his eulogy, one of my father's colleagues described him as, "a great inspiration, mentor, and friend." Who wouldn't want to be described that way by their colleagues?

For me, my father was the guy who was all in.

He was all in for his family, his friends, and his job. He didn't sit on the sidelines waiting for other people to get excited; he brought energy and passion into every situation.

My father really was that guy who—on his deathbed—really did wish he could have spent one more day at the office.

The numbers tell us that a lot of people are pretty miserable at work. It's time for us to change that. If you're reading this book, you have already decided that it is not ok to be miserable at work. You and your team deserve better than just going through the motions of a job. You deserve to do work that matters.

Why I Wrote This Book

If you're a CEO or senior leader reading this book, congratulations. You have the power to transform your organization and, in turn, the lives of your employees and customers. The biggest, boldest, fastest results occur when the CEO fully embraces a Noble Purpose mind-set and strategy. Whether you're accountable to a board, investors, or the market, you can be confident that the techniques in this book will improve your financial results, and your morale. It won't happen in a week, but it will happen.

If you're a not a senior leader, if you're somewhere in the middle, if you're just starting in your career, or you're a small entrepreneur, don't let your current position hold you back. In this book, you'll read examples of managers who have used purpose to transform departments and small work groups in ways that had a lasting and positive impact on the business results and the people involved. One launched a global initiative after a single manager put the concept forward. Noble Purpose is catching on because people are looking for ways to bring more meaning to their work.

If I do my job right, and you do your part, Noble Purpose will help you:

1. Find more purpose, passion, and meaning in your own job.
2. Help your team find more purpose, passion, and meaning in their jobs.
3. Improve your financial results exponentially.

There are lots of books telling you why you need a purpose. This book is different. Here, we'll go beyond aspiration—we'll dive into implementation. This is a step-by-step guide that shows you how to turn an ideal into an actuality. It's based on the work I've done with large clients like Google and Roche, as well as smaller firms like a concrete company in Omaha, and an accounting firm in Atlanta.

Noble Purpose is the new narrative of business. It will enable you to deliver better results, and become the kind of leader people want to follow. People want to make money. They also want to make a difference. Leading with Noble Purpose enables you to do both.

PART I

The Noble Purpose Leader

Our prime purpose in this life is to help others.

—Dalai Lama

1

Profit is Not
a Purpose

When I grow up, I want to claw my way into middle management.
— Said no 10-year-old, ever

Do you remember the Monster.com Super Bowl ad?

Monster's iconic "When I Grow Up" campaign featured kids saying, "When I grow up I want to be a Yes-man" or "Yes-woman" "Yes, sir. Anything for a raise sir." The Monster ads juxtaposed the dreams of childhood with realities of adult work. Watching an earnest 10-year-old boy say, "When I grow up, I want to claw my way into middle management," reminded people, work was supposed to be better than this.

The rise and fall, and subsequent rebirth, of Monster.com illustrates why a profit focus erodes business, while a purpose focus brings the business to life. Monster.com was founded on the belief that helping people find jobs was a noble endeavor. In their iconic ads, Monster made it clear: "You deserve a better job, and we want to help you find it." Monster founder Jeff Taylor's mantra was "It's half about a better job, and half about a better life." In 2006, Monster.com was one of the 20 most visited websites in the world.

Yet by January of 2011, five years later, Monster Inc. was rated the worst stock of the year. By 2014, things were worse. In that year alone, Monster's shares dropped 43 percent.

What went wrong?

Analysts suggested that Monster's free fall was due to their inability to compete with newer, more nimble, connected solutions like Indeed and LinkedIn. The analysts were right about the outcome, but they missed the root cause. Lack of competitive differentiation and old technology were only symptoms. The root cause for Monster's free fall was they lost their purpose.

In 2007, after Taylor and his team had left, Sal Iannuzzi became the CEO of Monster worldwide. Iannuzzi preached a very different message from Taylor's. Iannuzzi didn't talk about job seekers, or helping people find better lives. Instead, he put the focus on earnings. Without a leader to champion the cause, over time Monster's original noble purpose—helping people have better lives—eroded.

Iannuzzi's Town Hall meeting in June of 2014 illustrates the problem. Monster's stock was at an all-time low. Iannuzzi was announcing the launch of a new strategy and a global rebrand that were intended to reverse their decline.

When Iannuzzi took the stage at Monster headquarters in Weston, Massachusetts, to announce his plans, 800 employees were sitting in the auditorium, and over 4,000 more employees dialed in via webcast from 36 countries around the globe. The employees knew their company was at a critical juncture. Would they be hearing about a new strategy that would jolt their business back to life?

As Iannuzzi began, he talked about the need to increase earnings saying, "Our number one responsibility and focus is increasing shareholder value. That will pay us, that's why we're here." He hammered on the point saying, "That's what we're here to talk about. Everything you're going to hear [today], the emphasis is on how we're going to do that."[1]

The rest of Iannuzzi's presentation was a blur of numbers that concluded quickly. Not once during the entire presentation did

---

[1] Thompson Reuters StreetEvents:, "MWW: Monster Worldwide Strategy Briefing Day," edited transcript, May 14, 2014.

Iannuzzi talk about Monster's aspirations for job seekers. There was no mention of better jobs and better lives. Instead, he told his team, the single goal of their new strategy was to increase the stock price. Not help customers, not improve the industry, just increase the earnings. Afterwards, one attendee said, "It was as though the oxygen was slowly leaving the room."

When original Monster.com founder Jeff Taylor talks about his time at Monster he says, "The pride of helping millions of people find jobs was real inside the company. We read testimonials from people all over the world at our meetings. It was meaningful."

Iannuzzi's narrative about stock price never touched on pride they might derive from helping people. His presentation at the Town Hall was consistent with the way he routinely discussed Monster in the press. For example, he said to the *Wall Street Journal* in May of 2012, "I owe it as part of my fiduciary responsibility to increase shareholder value any way that I can. That's what the process is all about." This was same story he emphasized on a daily basis to his employees.

Sadly, Sal Iannuzzi is not unique. He's an exaggerated version of what happens in conference rooms and boardrooms every day. How many other leaders have had the same conversation with their teams? How many board meetings and departmental meetings have been exclusively focused on earnings with few or no conversations about customers?

Iannuzzi's focus on earnings was understandable. Like all CEOs, he was under pressure to drive the numbers. He might not be a bad guy. Yet he made a common leadership error. He focused on profit instead of purpose. In doing so, he eroded the driving force that had once made Monster great. Their business was no longer about making people's lives better; it was about making money, end of story.

Monster serves as a cautionary tale. The same scenario could have just as easily happened elsewhere. In fact, it already has. Companies like Blackberry, Blockbuster, Sears, and Toys 'R' Us, who were once giants in their spaces, took gut-wrenching tumbles when they lost their sense of purpose. It wasn't a loss of earnings that caused the loss of purpose; it was a loss of purpose that caused earnings to decline. In each of these organizations, the leaders were so intent on making money from their existing business model that they lost sight of their companies' true purpose: to improve their customers' lives. With no lens on the customer's world, they were outinnovated, outsold, and outmaneuvered. By focusing on profit instead of purpose, they became dinosaurs.

Under Iannuzzi's leadership, Monster's stock value declined by over 90 percent. Between April of 2007, when he was named CEO, and November of 2014, when he departed, Monster lost 93 percent of its market capitalization, falling from 5.5B USD to under 400M USD. Analysts said he was fired for declining stock value. Insiders know the loss of purpose came first. Fortunately, the Monster story does not end there. Iannuzzi's successor, CEO Timothy Yates, a long-time Monster employee, is taking a decidedly different approach. Yates launched an "All the Jobs, All the People," strategy focused on helping job seekers. Later in this chapter you'll learn how Monster is reigniting their true noble purpose.

The idea that a leader's primary purpose is to drive earnings is pervasive in many, if not most, organizations.

Unfortunately, It's Also Wrong

Compare the typical "let's rally around earnings" message with the words of these leaders:

- Ryan Holmes, Founder and CEO of Hootsuite, the social media management system that has exploded globally, kicks off their Town Halls saying, "We're more than a social media company. *We empower our clients to turn their messages into meaningful relationships.*"
- Steve McHale, the CEO of Explorys, the health care intelligence cloud company that has built one of the largest clinical

data sets in the world, says, "We unlock the power of big data to improve healthcare for everyone."

- Bruce Poon Tip, founder of Toronto-based G Adventures, who has become the global leader in adventure travel, says, "Our business model transcends our products. We're not just a travel company, *We help people discover more passion, purpose, and happiness.*"

As you read the statements these leaders use to describe their businesses, ask yourself, *Who would you rather work for?* A boss who tells you that your sole purpose is to deliver earnings for shareholders? Or a boss who tells you that your true and noble purpose is to make a difference in the lives of your customers?

These three leaders have absolute clarity about how they make a difference in the lives of their customers, as does every member of their organizations. The results speak for themselves:

- Hootsuite has grown 56,000 percent over the past five years. That is not a typo—fifty-six thousand percent. Even after their initial explosion, in the last 24 months they have more than doubled their business.
- Explorys has experienced unprecedented growth year-over-year. The year after they launched their purpose with their team, they grew revenue by 53%. They now work with 26 major healthcare networks, delivering care to 50 million unique patients at 360 hospitals.
- Bruce Poon Tip and his team of "Global Purpose Specialists" (the name adopted by his sales force) have grown revenue by 25 percent every year for the 25 years they've been in business. They're now a $400 million company. Since implementing Noble Purpose in 2013, they've accelerated their growth rate to 35 percent.

These leaders are early adopters. They're also our clients. You'll read more about how these three leaders and others have driven exponential growth, leveraging the power of purpose. For now, think about the way these leaders talk about their businesses.

You can tell a money story, or you can tell a meaning story. Think about your own business. Is the driving question, How can we make more money? Or, is the driving question, How can we make a difference to our customers?

As a leader, you're the one who tells your team why the organization exists. In *Selling with Noble Purpose*, I said, "If you treat your customers like a number, they'll return the favor." Now, we'll take it a step further. If you treat your employees like a line item, they'll pay you back in kind. They'll regard you, their jobs, your customers, and your entire organization as expendable resources, something they dispose of the moment something better comes along. Instead of emotional engagement, you'll be left with a transactional relationship, which will permeate every aspect of your organization, including your relationship with customers.

The internal conversation becomes the external conversation. When your story is exclusively focused on financial metrics, you drive towards mediocrity. It's counterintuitive. It's also true. Internal financial metrics do not create a competitive differentiation. A story about profit, revenue, and share price will never jump-start innovation, improve customer service, or inspire employee loyalty.

Purpose Drives Profit, Not the Other Way Around

To illustrate how powerful purpose can be, let's look at a side-by-side comparison. While Sal Iannuzzi and other *show me the money* leaders were telling their teams that increasing shareholder value was their primary goal, Mike Gianoni, CEO of Blackbaud, was telling his team a different story.

Blackbaud is in the tech space, they're a cloud company. They're a firm based in Charleston, South Carolina, that serves the philanthropic community. They describe themselves this way: "Blackbaud combines software and service to help organizations achieve their missions." Their clients include the Salvation Army, The Red

Cross, and thousands of smaller nonprofits. Blackbaud works in over 60 countries to support more than 30,000 customers.

When Mike Gianoni took over as President and CEO in January of 2014, Blackbaud was the market leader. But their stock price was declining, and their earnings were flat. They were seeing early indications that clients were frustrated with lack of updates to their products. Contracts that were once secure were going out for bids. Recurring revenue was dropping.

Many CEOs would have jumped in to rally their team around increasing revenue. Instead, Gianoni chose a different focus. Despite the stock market pressure every CEO feels, Gianoni didn't lead with numbers; instead, he started talking about Blackbaud's clients. Not just who the clients were, but also what they did, and the impact they were having on their constituents and communities.

Gianoni describes the way Blackbaud had traditionally run their staff "All Hands" meetings, "When I first started with the company, for the most part, leaders would stand on the stage, and in a one-hour meeting they would spend 45 minutes on the financials."

Blackbaud's previous leadership had focused on the money story, not the meaning story. Gianoni flipped it. He says, "Now I only spend five minutes on the financials." The new format is, "What's our purpose, how does our work impact clients, are we being effective in serving them, and are we doing okay financially?"

Gianoni says, "It's more important to have our associates understand why we get up and go to work each day. At the end of the day, if you have a healthy culture, if everyone is focused on client success, if your leadership is made up of the right leaders, who have integrity and are building a team that is focused on delighting clients, and our culture reflects decisiveness and an action-orientation, when all that happens, the financials fall into place. The financials are at the bottom of that, not at the top of that."

He says, "That's how companies actually work, that's why we do our All Hands meetings that way."

Gianoni recognized the truism, that profit and other quantitative metrics are lagging indicators. Qualitative metrics like what gets discussed at meetings, how do managers coach, and customer success are what ultimately drive the financial results.

Gianoni started bringing customers into All-Hands meetings. At one meeting, the director of the Wings for Kids program described how her organization teaches emotional intelligence to struggling kids, and the impact it has on their lives. She explained how Blackbaud's software enables them to serve more kids, and raise money, in more effective ways.

Gianoni says, "In that moment, the engineer who built that solution is sitting there saying, 'I helped create something that is making a positive difference in the world.' That's what people go home and talk to their spouses about. They don't go home and talk about EBIDAT and stock price. That's for me and Tony [CFO Anthony Boar] to worry about."

Over the course of a year, the cadence and tone at Blackbaud shifted. Vice President of Sales Patrick Hodges says, "Now we spend more time talking about customer impact than stock price. That's a change from the way it was before Mike joined. The senior leaders still cover stock price. Yet people walk away from the meeting, thinking, 'Damn, I am glad we are doing well, and look how we are helping all these organizations.'"

Hodges's team, which is part of the General Markets Business Unit, articulated their aspirations for their clients by crafting their own purpose statement, "We accelerate your Noble Purpose." One salesperson said, "When our software helps these organizations raise more money, and run their operations more successfully, we are literally helping humanity around the entire world." Hodges says, "In sales you have to get your people feeling good and excited about it. That's half the battle."

Hodges began a weekly *Sell it Forward* email, spotlighting a different client each week. Hodges asked the salespeople to describe clients by answering these questions: *What's the client's mission? What's their ethos? What are their values?* He asks them to describe the impact their solutions have on their clients: *How will this client be better as a result of doing business with Blackbaud? How will the success of our project impact their mission?* Salespeople began to compete to have their clients included. Hodges' *Sell It Forward* emails started spreading across the organization. He was the internal champion who stuck to it week after week.

Gianoni was an avid reader of the Sunday night emails. He would often comment, forwarding along his enthusiasm and compliments for the way Blackbaud was helping their clients fulfill their mission and purpose.

Product development people began to look forward to hearing about clients' organizations. One Sunday night, Hodges' son was ill, and he didn't send the regular email. First thing Monday morning, a product development manager marched into his office, saying, "Where's the email? I need it for my weekly meeting." The product development team was sharing the stories each week; it gave them pride in their jobs, and fueled them to be more innovative. They were motivated to help these clients in bigger, bolder ways. In that moment, Hodges realized that his emails were doing more than just motivating his team, they were engaging everyone.

The *Sell It Forward* emails served as an ongoing sharing system that kept customer impact at the front of the organization on a weekly basis. The marketing team used the customer-impact stories to create more compelling collateral. One year later, when they launched a new product the marketing team focused on how the software would help their clients better accomplish their missions. Hodges says it was a totally different launch, "In the past, we would have spent most of the time on the technical features. Instead, this launch was about client impact, and how we could give our customers the ability to do more good for those they serve."

Eighteen months after Gianoni joined Blackbaud, the organization has an entirely different ethos. They've captured more market share. They've successfully launched a new product. Recurring revenue now exceeds 75 percent of total revenue for the first time in the company's history. That means Blackbaud is keeping their clients and gaining new ones. They have a stable revenue stream that allows them to be even more innovative in the future.

And the ultimate proof: Under Gianoni's leadership Blackbaud's stock rose from $37 a share to $60 a share, as of this writing (see Figure 1.1).

Blackbaud's results reveal how a purpose-focus versus a profit-focus plays out over time across an organization.

Medicore and high-performing leaders focus on earnings and internal metrics. Gianoni and other high performing leaders focus on customers and external impact. While others in his space were talking about money, Gianoni talked about meaning. The difference in results is night and day.

As a post Ianuzzi update on Monster, when I originally wrote about Monster's loss of purpose for Forbes.com, several Monster employees posted comments about their disappointment that their business seemed to have lost its soul. The article circulated through Monster, and as you can imagine, they weren't pleased. Imagine

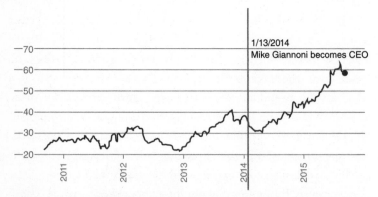

Figure 1.1   Blackbaud's Stock Pre- and Post-Mike Gianoni's Purpose-Driven Leadership

my surprise when several months later Yates and his senior advisors wanted to meet with me to discuss how Monster can reignite their team around a larger purpose. I've now shifted from critiquing Monster to working with them. Yates and his team are authentic in their desire to help Monster reclaim their mojo, and I'm all in to help them.

Their new narrative is focused on job seekers. During a recent earnings call, Yates shared a tweet from a senior human resources executive at a major technology company, who tweeted out "@Monster—congratulations on getting your sexy back, impressed by your new products and services." I'm all in for Monster. Reversing their results will not happen overnight. But as Mike Gianoni demonstrated at Blackbaud, when the leader puts purpose front and center, the cadence and tone change, the emotional undercurrent shifts, and the financial results follow.

You may be thinking at this point, I'm not the CEO. What can I do?

Let's look at another scenario. What if instead of being CEO, Gianoni had been a mid-level manager, and he had a *show me the money* peer in the same organization? What if they were both running product development teams? Whose team would be more innovative? What if both were managing big plants, or marketing groups, or sales teams? Whose team would be more emotionally engaged? The leader who talked about money, or the leader who talked about meaning? Whose team would be more dialed in to customers? Who would attract better talent? At the end of two years, which of the two leaders do you think would have better results?

It's tempting to think a high-minded concept like Noble Purpose doesn't apply to people down in the trenches. In our experience, with firms large and small, with individual leaders and CEOs, the results play out in similar fashion, irrespective of size or scope.

Here's how a summary of a profit focus versus a purpose focus plays out over time across an organization.

Action/Event	Profit-Driven	Purpose-Driven
The driving question:	How can we deliver more earnings?	How can we create more value for customers?
CEO message to employees	Your purpose is to increase shareholder value.	Your purpose is to make a difference in the lives of our customers.
Leadership questions	How can we make more money? How can we beat the competition? How can we hold our people more accountable for our metrics?	How do we make a difference? How do we do it differently than our competition? On your best day, what to you love about your job?
Lobby plaque	Our mission is to achieve market leadership and provide a return to our shareholders.	Our Noble Purpose is to improve the lives of our customers.
Board of directors emphasis	Short-term earnings for stockholders/ owners	Long-term value for customers and market
Leadership focus	Quarterly earnings Bonuses Stock price Efficiency measures	Company values Customer impact Industry innovation Employee engagement
Profit	Our end game	A critical measure of how well we're performing against our purpose

Action/Event	Profit-Driven	Purpose-Driven
Typical projects	"Big Lean"—A company-wide initiative to strip costs out of the system. Objectives: ■ Reduce product costs ■ Reduce overhead ■ Improve efficiency ■ Intensify vendor requirements	"Noble Knights"—A task force devoted to improve customer impact Objectives: ■ Improve product quality ■ Enhance customer experience ■ Create KPIs to measure progress against our purpose ■ Improve vendor partnerships
Relationship with vendors	Transactional at best; adversarial at worst Driven by price and terms Meetings to dictate demands Get the best price today	Mutually beneficial Collaborative Focus on customer impact Meetings to generate ideas Create value for both parties
Buzzwords	Cost reduction Lean Accountability	Customers Noble Purpose Passion
Employee focus	Work feverishly to reduce costs and increase earnings	Work feverishly to create value for customers

(Continued)

Action/Event	Profit-Driven	Purpose-Driven
Sales focus	Kill the competition Close sales faster Improve margin	Create competitive differentiation Understand customer goals Improve customer impact
Month three results	Earnings are up Efficiency measures have taken costs out Programs are working Employee engagement flat Sales close ratio flat	Everyone understands our purpose All departments know who our customers are and the impact they have on them Customer impact stories shared broadly A few new sales wins due to differentiated story Employee engagement on the rise Revenue and profit likely unchanged
Main topics in meetings	Internal numbers How can we beat last quarter's earnings? How can we become more profitable?	External customer impact How can we do even better for our customers? How are our customers responding?
How management reports results	We collected this much revenue	We helped this many customers
Customers discussed as:	Numbers	People whose lives and businesses matter

Action/Event	Profit-Driven	Purpose-Driven
Marketing message	Feature Benefits Pricing	Customer impact Compelling stories Value
Performance Evaluations	What have you done for us lately?	What are you doing for our customers?
Key metrics	Profit Earnings Productivity	Customer impact Customer retention Employee engagement in addition to profit, earnings, and productivity
Product development focus	What can we do to increase margins on our products and services? How can we beat the competition?	What can we do to add more value to customers? What's going on inside the lives and businesses of our customers? Think big, think crazy.
Customer service focus	Reduce costs Decrease call times Employees have little authority to provide solutions	Solve customer problems Employees have authority to make it right
Internal communication themes	Flavor of the month Ever changing rah-rahs Earnings reports Generic value proposition	Constant reinforcement—We make a difference—even when times are tough Our customers are counting on us

(Continued)

Action/Event	Profit-Driven	Purpose-Driven
Manufacturing	How much did you make? What did it cost? How could you do it cheaper?	How do our customers rate our products? How can we be better than our competition? Why does your role matter?
Distribution	How cheaply did you get it there?	What can we do to improve the customer experience?
Six-month results	Products the same, or cheapened Customer experience same or declined No compelling sales narrative Employees weary of constant pressure for earnings	Product development breakthroughs Customer loyalty increasing New sales won due to differentiated story and actions Employees are turning into True Believers
Typical motivational quote	"Show me the money!" —*Jerry Maguire*	"Profit isn't the purpose of a business, it's the test of its validity." —Peter Drucker
Sales mantras	Sell the customer, whether he needs it or not	Help customers achieve their goals
Sales manager questions	When will you close it? How big will it be?	How will this customer be different as a result of doing business with us?
CRM focus	Pipeline management	Customer intelligence plus pipeline

Action/Event	Profit-Driven	Purpose-Driven
Marketing collateral	Product features and price	Customer impact stories that include emotion
Favorite cartoons	*Dilbert*	*Dilbert* (it reminds us of the competition)
Production focus	Efficiency	Quality
Most frequently used words	ROI, cost efficiency, productivity	Customer impact, product relevance, differentiation, creativity, innovation
12-month results	Revenue flat Early indicators of customer churn Reduced margins due to lack of differentiation	Revenue trending upward Average customer spend increasing Winning deals away from competition without cutting price
Challenges	Low employee engagement Low customer engagement	Keeping up with demand Staffing to meet growth needs
Customer relationships	Transactional	Symbiotic—both parties need and value the other
Leadership style	Punish mistakes Reward quick wins	Okay to take risks—75 percent success rate means you're stretching
Culture at 18 months	We make money	We make a difference

(*Continued*)

Action/Event	Profit-Driven	Purpose-Driven
Market perception	Perceived as a commodity Top talent starting to leave	Clearly differentiated Becoming a destination employer
18-month results	Customers leaving Earnings lagging Stock declining	Customers calling Earnings increasing Stock increasing

2

Are You Telling a Money Story or a Meaning Story?

No business needs to be a commodity business competing only on price.
Every business can market itself based on its personality and spirit—in
other words, its soul.

— David Lapin, *Lead by Greatness*

Imagine you just boarded an airplane and took your seat. As you're settling in, your seatmate arrives. After a few pleasantries, he asks, "What do you do?" Oh no, it's elevator speech time. How would *you* answer?

Most people answer with their role. They say things like, "I'm an accountant," or "I'm in sales." Others answer with their industry: "I'm in medical equipment," or "I run a travel company."

It's the standard airplane conversation, but it rarely inspires anyone. Unfortunately, it also represents the way most people experience their jobs: an endless list of responsibilities, uttered with a weary sigh, and completely devoid of passion.

But what if your seatmate asked a completely different type of question? What if he asked: "Can you tell me about when you made a difference to someone at work?"

How would you answer that question? Do you ever remember a time when what you do for a living made a meaningful contribution to someone specific?

What if you were a senior executive for a corporate travel management company and you answered: "Last week a representative for a large manufacturing company was in Bangkok scoping new sites. Her flight was cancelled; she didn't speak the language; she had to get home. She called us, and we got her home within 24 hours."

"Wherever they are in the world, if people get stuck, or if they have trouble, they call us. If they need to go somewhere to close a deal or expand their business, they call us. I work for the most incredible company. We allow people to do business around the world. We are part of the economic engine, we facilitate economic expansion. In my job, I get to make people around the world feel like they're part of something amazing."

The above answer isn't imagined, it's real.

That's the way Gregory Lording describes his job. Lording is the Global Brand Manager for FCm Travel Solutions, a corporate travel management company that is part of the world's largest travel agency, Flight Centre, based in Brisbane, Australia. Lording and the other 18,000 Flight Centre employees around the world are part of a growing tribe of people who have decided to create a more meaningful experience at work.

These people don't work for nonprofits, they're not feeding the poor, and they're not forgoing their wages. They work in for-profit companies, in industries like accounting, manufacturing, consulting, and others. They make a good living, *and* they've created meaningful workplaces by focusing on the positive impact they have on customers. They live and breathe their Noble Purpose.

At first glance, businesses like corporate travel, manufacturing, or accounting might not be the sexiest things in the world. But they make the wheels of commerce spin. The people who buy these products and services use them to bring beauty, efficiency, safety, fun, and other real benefits into their lives.

Let's go back to you on the airplane. How would you react if someone described their work to you in the way that Lording describes his role? Do you think he's crazy, or would you want to know more? Do you want to do business with people who are that excited about their jobs? Or do you assume they're merely spewing the company line?

Now for the harder questions: When was the last time you described your own job in such a passionate way? What about your team? Do the people in your organization believe that their work makes a difference?

Make no mistake; people like Gregory Lording and the other purpose-driven leaders who you'll meet throughout this book have tough jobs. Lording and his team at FCm work with procurement agents: people who are paid to play hardball on pricing and terms. FCm consultants deal with frustrated travelers, who call from the road during moments of high stress. Other leaders you'll meet deal with the stress of finance, the ups and downs of global production, and the complex regulations of heath care.

Yet despite challenges that could easily suck them into becoming negative or reactionary, these leaders have embraced a narrative and strategy to keep their teams focused on the big picture. For them, the big picture is about making a difference in their customers' lives.

Lording says, "It's about bringing the soul of your company to life."

Take those words in. When was the last time you heard a leader talk about her company's *soul?*

Lording says, "Noble Purpose embodies listening to the inner voice of your business. Then it magnifies across your company at lightning speed."

The year after they implemented Noble Purpose, Lording's team had record revenues. They closed bigger deals, and took business away from the competition. This isn't a coincidence.

The business case for purpose is clear. Now let's get personal.

Think about your own career. At work, when were you most engaged and happiest? If you're burned out right now, your heart might be yearning for the beach. But think back to a time when you felt excited and motivated. Was it a time when you were just trying to get a paycheck? Or was it a time where you knew that your work truly mattered? Were you trying to hit a productivity number, or were you excited about making a difference?

Numbers matter. Today's leaders have access to detailed reports that 20 years ago we could only dream about. But in an effort to be more rigorous, leaders often lose sight of the individual stories that drive emotional engagement. The story you tell about yourself and about your business becomes the story you tell your team about your business. It lives and breathes inside of them. It guides their daily actions. And, it ultimately becomes the story your team tells your customers.

As a leader, you have a choice: you can tell a money story, or you can tell a meaning story. Lording articulates: "Our work is more than just a corporate travel program; it's about the experience of the traveler themselves. Each trip is a significant event for that individual."

Lording continues: "Our Noble Sales Purpose is: *We care about delivering amazing travel experiences.*"

How would you like to do business with a company where every team member cares about you and your travel experience? How would you like to work for a company who tells you that their purpose is to care, and to deliver amazingly?

When Flight Centre rolled out their Noble Purpose initiative to their travel consultants around the globe, one tenured consultant came up to Lording and said, "I feel alive again." She compared it to traditional corporate initiatives saying, "I feel something is opening up in me, instead of something being stuck to me."

What happens to people when they feel something "opening up" in them at work? Is that person going to do more or less?

The answer is obvious. When the travel consultant said something was opening up in her, she was likely referring to a level of emotional engagement she hadn't experienced before.

Susan Fowler, the author of *Why Motivating People Doesn't Work and What to Do Instead*, says, "People don't understand the nature of their own motivation, so when they are unhappy at work, they ask for more money. They yearn for something different—but they don't know what it is—so they ask for the most obvious incentive: money. Managers take the easy way out and assume that since they can't comply with people's requests for more money, their hands are tied."

Your hands are not tied. As a leader, you have the power to give people what they're yearning for. They're yearning for a reason to show up for work.

Before Flight Centre launched their initiative project, their senior team came together to create their Noble Sales Purpose:

We care about delivering amazing travel experiences.

It's called a Noble Sales Purpose rather than simply purpose because it's crucial that every member of the organization understand that the products and services you *sell*, and what you get paid for, are instrumental in living the purpose. Each of the three words describes your intent:

Noble—It's in the service of others.
Sales—It's based on what you actually sell.
Purpose—It's your end game.

Your Noble Sales Purpose (NSP for short) is a short, compelling statement that answers what we call the three big discovery questions:

1. How do you make a difference to your customers?
2. How do you do it differently from your competition?
3. On your best day, what do you love about your job?

Creating a clear NSP insures that you and every member of your team have absolute clarity about how you make a difference in the lives of your customers. If you're already thinking about your own NSP, great. A strong NSP is the lynchpin of an effective Noble Purpose strategy. Before you create your own NSP, let's look at a few other examples and talk about how you're going to use your NSP.

You probably already have a good sense about how you make a difference to your customers. In Flight Centre's case, they had a strong sense of purpose *before* they created their NSP and launched their initiative. Their NSP statement took what was implicit in their business (caring about customers) and made it absolutely explicit.

Flight Centre founder and CEO Graham "Skroo" Turner has long said, "We open up the world for those who want to see it." To launch their initiative, the leadership team unpacked every aspect of their NSP. What does *caring* look like, in person, over the phone, and in policies? How could they *deliver* better and faster? How could they be more innovative, create better products? They've even created a course called "The Science of Amazing" to help their people understand what makes a trip amazing for different types of customers.

Each word of their NSP creates actions. By putting every element under scrutiny, they challenged themselves to be bigger and bolder; to live their NSP in every possible way.

Flight Centre Chief Operating Officer Melanie Waters-Ryan says, "You have to decide who you are and who you are not. This frees people of the need to operate in the transactional space." CEO Turner says, "If you can get it right, and people feel like they have a purpose at work, it has quite an impact."

To scale their global purpose initiative, Flight Centre pulled together a team they dubbed The Noble Knights. This team was a handpicked cross-section of leaders, one from each country. Carole Cooper, Flight Centre's Global Peopleworks Leader says,

"We wanted to get individual engagement and have action happen in that country. I know from many years of this, running it from Australia [their headquarters] wouldn't work. If you just do it in one country, you don't get the rest of the world engaged." Cooper and I worked with The Noble Knights to create roll-out plans for their respective countries.

Cooper's advice to other leaders is this: "Move quickly to get it imbedded within your organization. If everyone is saying the statement, that's a massive win."

Flight Centre's annual revenues are over $2.4 billion. They have 39 brands. Their businesses, including licensees, span 90 countries. They have over 18,000 employees. If a business of that size and scope can infuse a single purpose around the globe, you can infuse purpose in your business.

In his famous TEDx Talk, author Simon Sinek affirmed, "People don't buy what you do. They buy why you do it. And what you do simply proves what you believe."

Your NSP codifies what you believe. It makes it actionable for your team. It enables you to operationalize your aspirations. Your NSP is the jumping off point for creating a tribe of true believers who want to have the same impact on customers that you do.

Pointing yourself toward a larger purpose changes your field of vision in ways that affect multiple disciplines. An NSP lens on decision-making affects innovation, process improvement, manufacturing, and pretty much everything else in your business. You wind up creating better products and improving your systems and structure in ways that matter to customers.

Here's what we observe in our consulting practice: When leaders change their narrative, their team gets excited. When they put forth purpose-driven ideas, they get more buy in. Their teams become more creative, they go the extra mile, they start to think differently about the business. As the organization implements initiatives in alignment with their NSP, over time, earnings usually rise.

I say usually, because Noble Purpose is not a magic bullet. There is no such thing. Flight Centre COO Melanie Waters-Ryan says, "It doesn't solve other problems, it won't solve technical issues, it won't cover up bad practices. If you don't fix those, it won't work." Noble Purpose shines a light on areas of your business that may be out of alignment with your aspirations. Waters-Ryan says, "If you fix those, Noble Purpose adds to it brilliantly."

When you bring purpose to the fore, it will make everything else you do better. Purpose is not all that you need, but it will improve your other initiatives. Noble Purpose will not rescue a lousy strategy, but it will ignite a good strategy. It is a performance multiplier because it engages your most powerful resource, your people.

Flight Centre has some of the highest employee engagement scores in the world. Waters-Ryan says, "We as a brand need to give people something to be proud of. We need to show them where they add value. We need to help them feel even prouder of what they have."

People with purpose are proud of what they do. They talk to their friends and family about their job. They're excited to tell strangers about their company. Their kids understand what they do for a living. They talk about it at the dinner table. Their job is part of who they are.

After many years working in the purpose space, I've observed something interesting: when people talk about driving earnings or their bonus, they tend to look eager, and often tense. Yet when people talk about making a difference in the lives of their customers, their whole face lights up. They beam with pride.

The difference between these two experiences is startling. Try it yourself. Think about hitting your target for the year or quarter, where does your mind go? Imagine you hit it; you made the number. Do you feel excited to do more or simply relieved that you're done?

Now think about improving the life of a customer or colleague. How do you feel when you've accomplished that goal? It's a completely different experience. If you're like most people, you don't feel exhausted; you feel inspired. You're more energized, rather than less.

There's nothing wrong with being eager to hit a number. But what do you do after you hit the target? In most organizations, you keep moving the number up ever year. After a certain point, even the most motivated person grows weary of endlessly chasing a moving target.

Imagine two competing companies in similar industries; one has Noble Purpose, the other is more internally focused on profit and productivity metrics. In a market competition, the Noble Purpose company will win every time because they have the advantage of pride. When people are trying to hit a number, they're frantic, and they're frequently fear-driven.

Pride is different. When you're proud of the impact you're having on others, it motivates you to want more. When you're engaged in a cause bigger than yourself, your pride becomes self-sustaining. When you're chasing money, looking out across another year feels like starting over. When you ignite pride, each new year is an opportunity to build on the exciting things you're already doing.

Here's another personal observation. In my work with senior leaders I consistently notice that leaders who focus exclusively on earnings rarely smile. On the flip side, leaders who have a sense of purpose almost always smile; they have a spring in their step. CEOs trying to drive stock prices are usually looking toward their exit strategies; they want a way out of the business and want to take a big pile of money when they go. CEOs working for a larger purpose are playing a different game. They're excited to be *in* the business. It's no surprise, the purpose-driven CEOs I meet are generally happier and more well-liked than CEOs who focus on earnings. Their organizations are also ultimately more successful.

Money Follows Purpose

Revenue is a lagging indicator. Your revenue today reflects the decisions you made and the actions you took months ago. Your revenue 12 to 18 months from now will reflect the decisions you make today.

Several of the firms you'll read about achieved record years immediately following their implementation. In other cases it was more gradual. It's important to note that these firms don't ignore cost-cutting measures. They don't back away from tough decisions, and they launch multiple initiatives simultaneously. Earnings rise because every part of their organization is laser-like, focused on adding value to customers.

Here's what the difference looks like in practice:

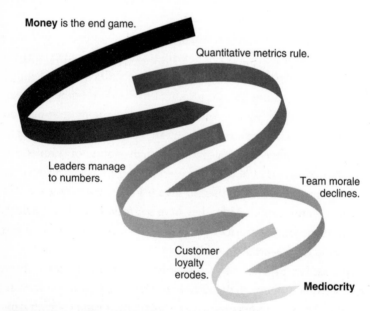

Money is the end game.

Quantitative metrics rule.

Leaders manage to numbers.

Team morale declines.

Customer loyalty erodes.

Mediocrity

Figure 2.1 The Low-Engagement Death Spiral—Mediocrity

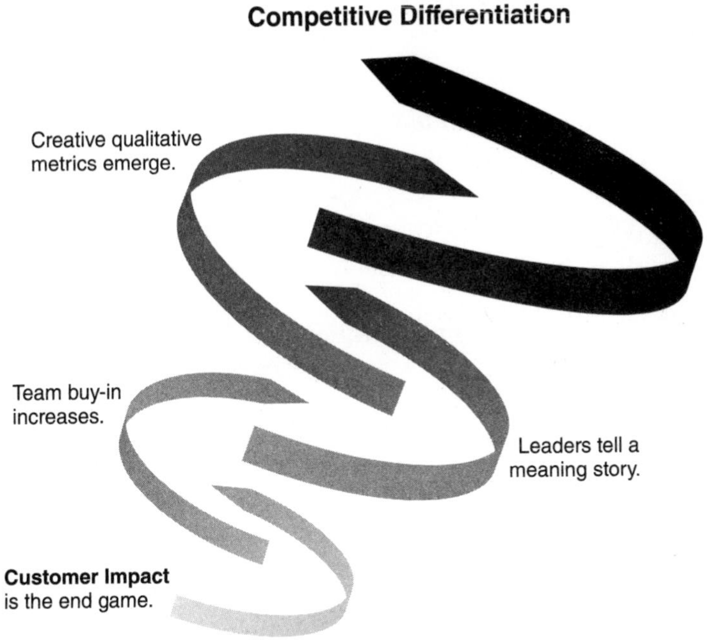

Competitive Differentiation

Creative qualitative
metrics emerge.

Team buy-in
increases.

Leaders tell a
meaning story.

Customer Impact
is the end game.

Figure 2.2   Purpose Drives Competitive Differentiation

Overemphasizing earnings erodes engagement, leading you down a death spiral towards mediocrity. A Noble Purpose focused on customer impact propels you to the high ground of competitive differentiation.

At this point, you might be saying, *I can't wait to jump in.* Or maybe you're thinking, *How do I start, where do I start?* Or perhaps you're wondering, *How am I going to get my bottom-line-oriented boss or board to go along with this?*

Consider this your playbook. First and foremost, Noble Purpose starts with you, the leader. You have to be clear about your *own* mindset and strategy before you implement projects with others. However, if you're like most Type As, you probably want to know where this is going, before you get introspective.

I tend to be impatient myself, so let me give you a teaser. There are five phases:

1. **Claim Your Noble Purpose**—Here is where you and your team will answer three big discovery questions. You'll clarify your customer identity, decide who is and who isn't your true customer, and prioritize your constituents. Then, informed by the three discovery questions and customer clarity, you'll craft your NSP.

2. **Prove Your Noble Purpose**—This step is about creating your narrative and the concrete substantiation behind it. You'll codify the impact you have on customers using stories and data. You and your team will identify compelling customer-impact stories. These are examples of what your NSP looks like in action, to demonstrate how your business affects the lives and businesses of your customers. You'll personalize your message. You'll prepare to explain why your purpose matters to you as the leader. You'll choose your Noble Purpose Accelerants, the quick wins and decisions that let the rest of your organization know you're serious about the process.

3. **Launch Your Noble Purpose**—Now it's time to win hearts and minds. In this phase, you'll activate Noble Purpose across all of your departments. Each team will identify the impact they have on customers, and how their work fits into the larger whole. Individuals will have a chance to connect your NSP to their roles and their own personal aspirations for their jobs. This phase is about helping your team internalize your strategy.

4. **Operationalize Your Noble Purpose**—This is where you bring your customers to life in every corner of your organization. Using visuals, stories, and key purpose indicators (KPIs), you'll bring customers to the fore in departments like finance, operations, customer support, and HR. You'll identify your Noble Knights to help you look at areas where you're already successful and can scale, as well as areas where you may be out of alignment. You'll start to infuse your Noble Purpose into your external messaging, sales aids, and marketing materials.

5. **Imbed Your Noble Purpose**—Here you'll establish systems and processes for ongoing reinforcement. You'll look at performance development and compensation. You'll challenge yourself to think creatively about customer retention. You'll look at how you solicit and review customer feedback. And ultimately, you'll look ahead to determine how you're going to create a legacy organization.

The above process represents what we know works. We weren't always this systematic. When we first began implementing Noble Purpose, it was more hit or miss, getting buy-in where we could and figuring things out along the way with our clients. I'm grateful to our early adopters, the clients you'll read about here. With their help, we codified the process into something others can replicate.

It's sequential, although not always perfectly linear. Each phase builds on the previous phase in a somewhat fluid manner. Some elements are done concurrently, and many are continuous. The Implementation Section at the end of this book outlines each step in a concise way so you can share it with your team.

Before we get to implementation, let's talk a little bit more about you. The strategic lens you have on your business and the words you choose to express it are critical. If you're not intentional about telling a meaning-story, your organization will default to a money-story because that's the traditional narrative of business.

You can have excellent products. You can give your employees a free organic lunch every day. You can put a pool table in your break room. But, as a leader, if you can't get people excited about your story, your business is doomed to mediocrity.

You don't have to be perfect. You don't even have to be charismatic. You simply have to give people a cause worth caring about.

3

How Metrics Drive Mediocrity

We must overcome the notion that we must be regular . . . it robs you of the chance to be extraordinary and leads you to the mediocre.

—Uta Hagen

We've all heard, "You can't manage what you can't measure."

The above quote is often attributed to Dr. W. Edwards Deming, the visionary business scholar who tr ansformed the auto industry.

But as a standalone, it's a misquote. When Dr. Deming said that, he used some pretty critical words before and after the statement that change its meaning entirely. According to the Deming Institute, Dr. Deming actually said, "It is wrong to suppose that if you can't measure it, you can't manage it—a costly myth."

This raises the following question: Why have so many people lifted out the middle of Deming's quote to emphasize the exact opposite of what Dr. Deming actually meant? The answer is twofold. The Deming Institute blog says, "Dr. Deming did very much believe in the value of using data to help improve the management of an organization." The blog suggests that the misquote is so frequently shared because, "The quote appeals to people seeing their organization fail to use data when they should be using data."

That's the logical well-intended reason. There's another, less obvious reason leaders default to the Deming misquote. Relying on data alone enables leaders to avoid the messy emotional work of actually leading. People fixate on lagging measures like revenue, profit, and productivity, because they're easy to track. But it's qualitative elements like customer impact, leadership language and emotional engagement that ultimately drive financial results. Said another way, the qualitative are the leading measures that predict the lagging quantitative measures like profit.

Dr. Deming never intended for people to focus exclusively on data. In fact, he stated that "Running a company on visible figures alone" was one of The Seven Deadly Diseases of Management. It's not without coincidence that number one and two on Deming's list of Deadly Diseases are lack of constancy of purpose and emphasis on short-term profit. Deming said, "The emphasis should be on why we do a job."

Dr. Deming understood the exponential value of pride. He said, "All anyone asks for is a chance to work with pride." Pride rarely springs from meeting externally-imposed mandates. Yet metrics-driven leadership has become the default because it's easier to scale than qualitative measures such as pride, passion, or purpose. Leaders set numerical goals to drive revenue, improve efficiency, and increase productivity. But as Deming and others have documented, metrics-driven leadership creates mediocrity at best, and active disengagement at worst.

The first step in becoming a Noble Purpose leader is to start looking at your business through a different lens. Managing to the numbers puts the emphasis in the wrong place.

One need look no further than our public school system to see how focusing exclusively on numbers can suck the soul out of even the most well-intended professional. Talk to any good public school teacher, and he or she will tell you that overemphasis on test scores has stripped the love of learning from our classrooms. Sadly, it's often the best teachers who are the most dispirited. My colleague and friend, Dr. Bob Patrick, an award-winning high school teacher says, "The current proliferation of testing and pressure now put on teachers only make the less capable teacher weaker, and the more capable teacher more likely to look for other work."

Take that in for a minute. Overemphasis on metrics is disheartening for top performers, and downright disabling for weaker performers. Dr. Patrick's comments about teachers plays out similarly in other organizations.

We've talked about the 51 percent of people who aren't engaged, and the 17 percent who are actively disengaged. Now let's talk about the 32 percent who actually are engaged in their work. They may like their jobs, but over time they pay a heavy toll for working with people who don't.

Three Trends That Make Purpose a Business Imperative

1. The Membership Economy

    People no longer buy brands; they join them. Robbie Baxter, author of *The Membership Economy* says, "Our relationship with organizations is shifting from ownership to access, from emphasizing the transactional to the relational, and from the traditional one-way communication from the organization to a multidirectional conversation."[1] This affects who we buy from, and who we choose to work for.

2. Forced Transparency

    Thanks to the anonymity and scope of the web, your internal beliefs seep out online. Customers and employees can read notes from your annual meeting online. Employees can post anonymous comments on Glass Door. Your competition can read your Yelp reviews. People are going to know what you stand for, whether you like it or not.

---

[1] Robbie Kellman Baxter, *The Membership Economy: Find Your Super Users, Master the Forever Transaction, and Build Recurring Revenue* (New York: McGraw-Hill, 2015).

3. Emotive Expectations

The emotional expectations of the self-help movement have moved into the workplace. Due in part to the rise of millennials in the workplace, today's top talent expect more than a paycheck and a 20-year path to a partnership. People want authenticity, fulfillment, and meaning from day one.

Managing to visible numbers alone creates a climate of disengagement. Poor performers remain poor performers, and they have a detrimental effect on top performers. Raj Sisodia, a co-founder of the Conscious Capitalism movement, describes the current state of employee engagement this way: "Imagine a 10-person rowing shell. Three people are rowing their hearts out, five people are just sitting there, and two people are hitting the others over the heads with their oars."

Sisodia's metaphor illustrates the following graphic (Figure 3.1) in a human way, to underscore the deep cost of disengagement. The monetary cost in the United States is currently estimated between $450 billion and $550 billion annually in lost productivity. The cost to the human spirit is even greater. Disengaged people have a chilling effect on everyone. If you've ever worked with people who are just phoning it in, you know how frustrating it can be. You find yourself thinking, *Why does our organization tolerate such mediocrity?*

As the number of disengaged employees escalates, trust in leadership declines.

Top performers either quit or leave. Or worse, they quit and stay. They become the people sitting in the boat just waiting for the race to be over.

This situation raises the question, *What are we going to do about it?*

Albert Einstein said, "We can't solve our problems with the same level of thinking that created them."

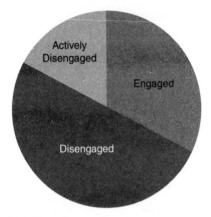

Figure 3.1   2014 Employee Engagement

To solve our engagement problem, we have to unpack the thinking that got us here. The mindsets that eroded workplace purpose have largely been unconscious. As data becomes more available, technology accelerates work's pace, and human connection suffers.

It wasn't a conscious decision, collectively or individually. There wasn't a caucus of leaders who decided to eradicate workplace meaning. But it happened. Much like you don't decide to put on 10 pounds, but with an abundance of food, a heavy work schedule, limited time to exercise, and the comfort of a good meal at the end of a long day, suddenly you turn around and (literally) there's the 10 pounds. You didn't plan it. But because you weren't intentional about staying healthy, on it went. **It doesn't happen by design, it happens by default.**

The same thing occurs in business. Companies grow larger, and people lose direct contact with customers. Organizations flatten, and leaders become responsible for more and more disparate areas. The stock market becomes more demanding, and the emphasis moves away from long-term value and toward a short-term earnings game.

Despite our efforts to become better, we become worse. In my work with organizations, I've observed that when purpose is absent, it's not by conscious choice.

Like that 10 pounds, it happens by default.

As Dr. Deming said, "A bad system will beat a good person every time." Managing solely to traditional metrics is part of an ineffective default system that erodes emotional engagement and competitive differentiation.

Can you imagine one of your service people telling a customer, "The thing I love about this company is that we hit all our productivity measures." Would the customer jump for joy and say, "Oh great, tell me more?" Of course not. Customers are interested in how you affect their businesses, not how you measure your own.

Picture one of your team members on the sidelines for their kid's soccer game. A fellow parent asks, "What's it like to work at your company?" Your colleague answers, "We're rigorous about numbers; every week we get a spreadsheet evaluating our performance." Would the other parent say, "Wow, that sounds great, are you all hiring?"

Numbers don't give your people anything meaningful to share with each other, or with anyone else for that matter. The other issue with numbers is that most companies use the exact same metrics as their competition. Using the same benchmarks as everyone else in your industry doesn't set the stage for competitive differentiation.

Reports track progress, but they're a snapshot, a backward-looking metric that reflects attitudes, beliefs, and behaviors that occurred months earlier. To be successful in today's fragmented, fast-paced world, you have to look at performance through a different lens.

Measuring Artistic Impression

People often ask, *How do you measure Noble Purpose?*

The short answer is, it's both cultural and systemic. If you're someone who has been managing to the traditional numbers for most of your career, expanding your field of vision can be challenging. To provide an example of a more holistic way to evaluate performance, let us turn for a moment to the world of competitive figure skating.

The figure skating competitions are consistently the most viewed events of the winter Olympics.

The scoring in figure skating is more complex than scoring in speed skating, or track. Figure skaters are scored on two elements. Part of the score is for technical merit, and part of the score is for artistic impression. If the scoring were simply based on technical merit alone, it would be a very boring event. If technical merit were the only thing that counted it would be one performer after the other doing the same jumps and turns with judges checking the boxes for technical proficiency.

It's the combination of technical merit and artistic impression that makes the competition so compelling. The top performers excel in both. They check all the boxes for technical merit, but those are just table stakes. Much like having a functioning product, or adequate services, it will get you into the competition. It might even get you into the finals. But no one wins gold on technical merit alone. The difference between silver and gold often comes down to the competitors' passion and how emotionally engaged they are in their own performance.

The same principle holds true in other sports: golf, tennis, soccer, and so on. Emotional engagement may not be as obvious in those events as it is with figure skating. Yet in every sport, the top winners are more than just technically proficient. They're passionate; they're emotionally engaged in their own performance. They're fully present for the game, and they care deeply.

Competitive differentiation in business is much the same. You have to meet the basic technical requirements to get into the game. True differentiation, however, stems from the more human, artistic elements. It's the hundreds of little things that contribute to the customer experience. It's the way your team pulls together after a mistake. It's the tone of voice from your customer service rep. It's your manufacturing team staying late to fix a problem. It's your product development manager thinking about your users when she's out for her morning run. It's your first-line manager caring enough to call a difficult customer, coach the struggling employee, and shine with enthusiasm on a rainy Monday morning.

HubSpot, the firm that reinvented inbound marketing, shares their Culture Code via a slide deck that says, "Balancing this dual personality of mission and metrics is challenging. But it's also partly what makes us different." The opportunity for differentiation is lost when leaders limit employee evaluation to things like: Did you cover all the elements in the five-step process? Did you hit all productivity metrics? Did you reduce the inventory by the appropriate amount? It becomes a check-the-box culture.

You'll create a better organization by asking things like: How are we improving the lives of our customers? How do we track and measure that? How does your performance impact our customers today, and tomorrow? What's our highest aspiration for our customers?

When quantitative measurements become the sole focus, it dulls down your organization. Employees quickly recognize that these types of metrics have little impact on anyone except the people measuring them. Quantitative measures are designed to improve compliance. Qualitative measures ignite commitment.

Implementing more holistic measures is crucial for taking your team to the next level. But don't be surprised if you face some resistance. There are three primary reasons organizations limit themselves to metrics-driven leadership. I've outlined them as follows, along with some strategies for overcoming each of these mindsets.

Use this list with your team to illustrate the imperative for moving beyond traditional metrics.

Numbers Feel Safe

Measuring and evaluating nuance takes judgment. Too often, leaders don't trust subordinates (or themselves) to make judgment calls. Organizations default to numbers because they assume that evaluating something as nuanced as emotional engagement is too difficult to measure. Except it's not.

Let's go back to figure skating. I've never skated; my knowledge of figure skating comes entirely from watching the Olympics. Yet with a minimal amount of training from sports commentators, I can usually pick the winners. I bet you can too. You know how to judge artistic impression.

People know great performance when they see it. Customers can tell when someone truly cares. Employees can tell when their coworkers are engaged and when they're not.

Noble Purpose organizations use nuanced qualitative evaluations because they know it separates the average from the exceptional. Google employees are evaluated on their Googliness. Top-tier private school teachers are evaluated on classroom engagement rather than just test scores. They have confidence that their leaders can tell the difference.

Elevating your metrics to include qualitative nuanced elements requires you to think about the impact you want to have on customers. You have to train your managers to understand your end game. Then you have to trust them to make judgment calls.

Fear about Fairness

When you open things up to qualitative interpretation, it's never going to be perfect. In an organizational setting, if you put forth a qualitative metric, like emotional engagement, or customer pride, and managers are able to rate it with even 75 percent accuracy, that's a huge improvement over not having it.

People may whine that it's too subjective. Too bad, you're going for success, not perfection. If you dumb the measurements down to the lowest level, you dumb the performance down to the lowest level.

The best organizations train their people to spot the nuances in attitude. They understand the difference between leading indicators and lagging indicators. They create systems to capture anecdotal customer comments. They expect leaders to look for deeper issues behind the surface numbers.

Nuance Takes Work

Numbers measure results; numbers do not create results.

Imagine a runner training for a big race. Everyday she goes out on the track, and her coach times her. He tells her the time. She runs again. He times her again. He produces weekly reports with her times. He does a comparison spreadsheet of her times versus the competition. He tells her, "You need to improve your time." Is she going to get better? Maybe. Timing her every day will make her *aware* of her results. But it doesn't equip her with any skills or techniques to improve.

Measuring performance is not leadership. A leader who only measures performance is like a mediocre junior high school gym teacher who stands there with a stopwatch clicking off times on the 50-yard dash, while she's counting down the minutes until sixth period.

The runner's current time reflects her *prior* training and coaching. If her coach wants her to improve, he'll need to unpack her technique, her mindset, and her habits, both on the track and off it.

He'll need to have a laser-like focus on the end game, and every step in between.

Noble Purpose leaders do more than measure performance; they create tools and techniques to improve performance.

To summarize, metrics-driven leadership drives mediocrity because:

- Metrics do not create a compelling narrative, internally or externally.
- Using the same benchmarks as everyone else will not create competitive differentiation.
- Numbers measure performance; they do not create performance.

Numbers tell a story, but it's yesterday's story. If you want to write tomorrow's story, you have to measure something different.

4

Go Beyond the Numbers

Measure what is measurable, and make measurable what is not so.
—Galileo Galilei

Hootsuite is a Vancouver-based SaaS company founded by Ryan Holmes in 2008. Holmes started the company when he needed a tool to manage multiple social media networks at his digital services agency, Invoke Media. Finding that there was no product in the market offering all the features he wanted, Holmes and his colleagues chose to develop a platform of their own. They're now the most widely used social relationship platform in the world. Their clients include Sony Music Entertainment, Adidas, eBay, Orange, Australia Post, AstraZeneca U.S., and Levi Strauss & Co. In 2015, they were named a top-rated Enterprise Social Media Management platform by software users on TrustRadius, the leading peer review site for business software.

Hootsuite's NSP is: *We empower our customers to turn messages into meaningful relationships.*

Holmes says, "Our purpose enables brands and consumers to take advantage and embrace social, allowing anyone to tap into its potential and revolutionize the way in which they communicate with their customers."

Chief Revenue Officer Steve Johnson joined the company as employee number 27 in North America. Johnson was an established technology executive who had been involved in a number of other fast-growth companies, as well as established firms like Constant Contact, Blackbaud, and Scopus. He joined Hootsuite because he believed in the power of social media. Holmes, Johnson, and the other leaders at Hootsuite have built a tribe of True Believers. Their offices aren't glamorous. Their Vancouver headquarters is interesting, with wood walls and owl-themed conference rooms. But it's far from fancy. They have big rooms filled with metal desks lined up right next to each other. There's little privacy. Employees who want to stand while they work don't get expensive standing desks or multiheight monitors like the cool kids in Silicon Valley. Instead, Hootsuite provides instructions for a $25 Ikea hack. You screw an Ikea shelf onto an Ikea end table, then stick the contraption on your desk to bring your monitor and keyboard to standing height.

Hootsuite doesn't provide free vegan lunches. They don't pay higher salaries. They don't offer unique benefits like sabbaticals or egg-freezing. Yet they attract and retain top tech talent because people are excited to be part of something they believe in.

Their team is on fire for the power of social media. Their challenge was getting clients to think bigger. Clients often only buy licenses for the social media or marketing team. Yet Hootsuite knew expanding the number of licenses per company would help their clients reach more customers and constituents in meaningful ways. Product differentiation wasn't enough. The team at Hootsuite wanted to drive exponential growth for themselves and their clients. Our strategy was to leverage compelling customer-impact stories.

Turning Techies into Storytellers

The Hootsuite team is competitive and they want to win. We leveraged their competitive spirit by launching a Story Off.

We started by training the customer facing teams to tell customer-impact stories. A compelling customer-impact story:

- Is true
- Is short—90 seconds or less
- Describes the impact your product had on a specific customer
- Includes vivid details
- Touches emotions
- Validates your NSP

The teams were coached and had plenty of time to practice. Then, they launched the Story Off. At their weekly team meetings, each manager had every member of their team share a customer-impact story. They recorded videos of each story with their iPhones. The first week was a practice week. After hearing everyone's stories, they gave each other feedback and coaching. The next week was a competition, where the team voted for the best story. They used the above bullets as their judging criteria. The winner for each team went to quarterfinals. The voting continued. The videos were shared company-wide giving everyone a chance to vote. The top five winners told their stories in front of the entire company at their Town Hall.

The Hurricane Sandy story was one of the most compelling. Dubbed the largest hurricane in diameter on record, Hurricane Sandy destroyed property and wreaked havoc up and down the East Coast, particularly in New Jersey. While the storm was downing trees and power lines—plunging neighborhoods into darkness—Morris County used their Hootsuite dashboard to prioritize pleas for help and send out rapid updates about road closures, evacuation efforts, and shelter locations. As authorities, news outlets, and individuals were left without power, for some, social media channels were the only choices for communication.

When the storm struck ground, the Morris County team responded directly to citizens as hundreds of tweets and Facebook comments came their way. At one point, when a group of people asked when their power might be restored, Carol Spencer, the digital and social media manager for Morris County, posted a message letting them know she had sent the information to Jersey Central Power & Light. This human response, enabled by Hootsuite, helped ease people's fears and proved that their county was really listening and doing its best to help them when they were in need. Managing their social media with Hootsuite gave Spencer and her team the power to build trust and meaningful relationships with vulnerable people during a dangerous situation.

Imagine you're a Hootsuite employee listening to this story. Your CEO has just told you that Hootsuite's Noble Sales Purpose is: *We empower our customers to turn messages into meaningful relationships.*

Then he invites an employee on stage to describe what happened during Hurricane Sandy. How do you feel about your company right now?

As the meeting progresses, you hear more customer-impact stories. You hear about how the Mall of America personally connects with shoppers to create better shopping experiences. You hear about school systems that use social media to reach out directly to parents and students. You hear about how small retailers are running contests via social media, to help them engage individually with customers. In an impersonal world, your software connects people in meaningful ways.

Are you getting what's happening here? Everyone in the company is hearing stories about how they're living their NSP.

Six months into their purpose initiative, Summer Recchi, Director of Sales Training, who worked on the project, sent this email:

> During Q2 Wrap Up presentation this morning, Steve [Johnson] told two customer stories before diving into the numbers. He also shared these two quotes at the end of his presentation:
> The Perfect Day.
> Going to bed with a dream, waking up with a purpose.
> "The purpose of life is not to be happy. It is to be useful, to be honorable, to be compassionate, to have it make some difference that you have lived and live well."
> —Ralph Waldo Emerson
> We have a purpose now. And we talk about it. It's changed us. It took a few months but it's finally happening!
>
> **Summer**

The above email from an astute observer of human behavior reveals what a change in culture looks like through the eyes of an employee. Chief Revenue Officer Steve Johnson is a high tech veteran; he's been part of many other successful organizations. He knows how to launch a team and grow revenue; he's done it before. He could have run the usual meetings, where they looked at numbers, and tracked progress. Hootsuite could have stuck with tracking deal size and time to close. They could have measured success in revenue. The market share was growing. People would have been happy to hear their results.

But they challenged themselves to go deeper. They added a qualitative metric—storytelling. They put a laser-like focus on it. They taught it, they coached it, they evaluated it, and they rewarded it. They brought it to the center of their daily operations. What's more, they didn't end it with the competition. It wasn't a one and done, flavor of the month initiative.

Johnson continues to share stories. Quarterly meetings include a section Johnson calls *Beyond the Numbers*. He says, "We've had mostly really good numbers, but what is more meaningful than that, is what our business means. We focus on customers and how we've helped them via our Noble Purpose." In addition to customer-impact stories, Johnson says, "I might also talk about a life framework, and ask people what impact they're having on the world."

Team members routinely tell Johnson that *Beyond the Numbers* is their favorite part of the quarterly meetings. The Hootsuite team have become excellent storytellers. Customer-impact stories are now part of the cultural DNA. They tell them to customers, prospective customers, and each other. In a world of techies spouting software features, Hootsuite's people stand out.

They've increased their deal size and shortened their sales cycle. In the last two years, they have more than doubled their revenue. CEO Holmes says, "My big task right now is how I build out the team to take us from 100 million in revenue, to take us to one billion. We'll have to solve a lot of pain from the market to build that out."

Hootsuite is not a me-too company. You can't establish market leadership by measuring the same things the rest of the market does. Hootsuite measures qualitative indicators like storytelling. Their quantitative key performance indicators (KPIs) are also unique to their purpose. Holmes says, "We measure engagement on message sends every day. That's a KPI that ties to our purpose."

Escape Me-Too Mediocrity

If you have an absolutely unique product, sometimes it can sell itself. When Steve Jobs stood on stage demonstrating the first iPhone, it was revolutionary. People waited in line to buy it. They paid a premium because there was no other product like it. That was then. Now, the iPhone has plenty of competition, and the product features are no longer as unique as they once were. Such is the life cycle of innovation; even if you have the coolest newest thing ever, it's only a matter of time before your competitor catches up to you. It's also worth noting that when he launched the original iPhone, Steve Jobs still had a story. He didn't present the product using a spec sheet.

When I work with organizations who are finding themselves commoditized, I almost always observe that an absence of customer-impact knowledge is apparent. They tend to use side-by-side comparisons of their features versus their competitors to demonstrate their value. But it backfires. It takes the customer into the weeds. You wind up even more commoditized because you've encouraged customers to attach a monetary value to each individual feature.

Customer impact is a more effective way to demonstrate value.

Dig into the Nuances

Being the best at the same thing everyone else is measuring is not going to wow anyone. Can you imagine if Disney benchmarked themselves against other theme parks? They don't. They measure themselves against their own purpose—are we creating magic for guests? Innovation expert Steve Shapiro, the author of *Best Practices Are Stupid*, says, "You can't benchmark against someone in your industry. If you're differentiated you should have different benchmarks."

Noble Purpose organizations measure different things, they dig deeper into the nuance. For example, Chick-fil-A, the Atlanta-based chicken chain, is the country's favorite fast food establishment according to the latest customer satisfaction survey from the American Customer Satisfaction Index (ACSI).

In an industry where speed and efficiency (and occasionally food quality) are the industry benchmarks, Chick-fil-A goes further. Most fast food chains look at customer ratings, but Chick-fil-A reads every single comment on their customer comment cards.

That's because Chick-fil-A knows that customer comments reveal what people are *really* thinking. While revenue is a lagging indicator, customer comments are a leading indicator. Comments provide the nuance. Are they harder to measure and track? You bet they are. Qualitative information is always harder to interpret. It's also where you get the best feedback about your culture and the impact you have on your customers.

Ignoring nuanced qualitative elements puts your organization at risk because it makes it more difficult to engender customer trust. As marketing guru Seth Godin says, "You don't get trusted if you're constantly measuring and tweaking and manipulating so that someone will buy from you. I don't have any problem with measurements, per se; I'm just saying that most of the time when organizations start to measure stuff, they then seek to industrialize it, to poke it into a piece of software, to hire ever cheaper people to do it."

The best organizations recognize differentiation requires nuance.

5

Make Your Customers Human

Business is the fundamental endeavor of human life, it is the primary place and context in which we enact our humanity.
                    —Steve Overman, *The Conscious Economy*

As the world grows bigger and companies get larger, there are more layers between the people who work in an organization and the market. The very fact that we use the phrase "the market" to describe customers is emblematic of the problem. The people whose lives a company is serving become abstracted, generalized, and fragmented. They become aggregated transactions, instead of individual human beings.

For example, look at health care. Cost-cutting measures tend to dominate the conversation, and the push for efficiency is relentless. Patients are discussed as clinical outcomes. It's ironic that in one of the most intimate industries, the connection to individual human beings is often lost.

This happens in all industries. Yet the further removed people are from customers, the more likely they are to see them as objects rather than humans. As a leader, your job is to humanize the customers for everyone in the organization.

Bringing Patients to Life

Explorys, the health care intelligence cloud company you met in Chapter 1, was founded in 2009 as an innovation spinoff from Cleveland Clinic. Originally inspired by physicians and informatics leaders, Explorys combines healthcare computing platform solutions for clinical integration, at-risk population management, cost of care measurement, and pay-for-performance solutions.

If it sounds complex, that's because it is. Explorys has a direct impact on the lives of patients. But as a cloud company whose product is analytics and big data, the Explorys team doesn't work directly with patients. Even further, many of their coders, data scientists, and high tech experts tend to be young and healthy. A group of high tech wizards in their 20s and 30s typically haven't experienced healthcare first hand, other than the occasional ER visit. Additionally, the majority haven't had to deal with aging parents.

The core leadership team cofounders, CEO Steve McHale, President Charlie Lougheed, and Chief Medical Officer Anil Jain, along with the VP of Marketing and Sales Sarah Mihalik, wanted to ensure that everyone in the organization understands the impact their work had on individual people.

Mihalik says, "We are bringing together the convergence of payers, providers, and life science to change healthcare." Mihalik shared a story to illustrate the impact Big Data can have on an individual person. She says, "Picture two men. One is Joe, the other is Mike. Joe and Mike are both 55, they both work the night shift at local factories. They're both a little overweight, and they both have diabetes.

Joe is the father of two boys, one in college, and one in high school. Every night he goes to work, and then he comes home to sleep while his kids are at school, so he can spend evenings with them. Joe tries to take care of himself and maintain a healthy lifestyle, but he struggles. With his late shifts, and his family commitments, it's difficult to exercise and eat healthy. He hasn't been in to see his doctor in quite a while. He's so tired when he gets off work, scheduling a routine checkup is the last thing on his mind.

Joe's youngest son is a basketball player. Joe goes to all his games. His son's team is in the running for the state championship. Joe is super dedicated to his son, and does everything he can to be there for him.

One night at work, Joe starts feeling badly. He gets dizzy, he passes out. He's taken to the ER where they realize Joe's kidney function is failing so badly that he needs to start dialysis. Joe misses six weeks of work trying to get his kidney function up. And worst of all, Joe misses his son's championship game. Joe survives, but his health is forever compromised."

"It didn't have to be this way," says Mihalik. She explains to her team how a similar scenario plays out differently for Mike, the other 55-year-old man who works the late shift in a factory. "Like Joe, Mike is a diabetic whose hours and family commitments make it hard for him to take care of himself. But Mike's healthcare provider uses Explorys' Big Data to track trends, and to track Mike's interactions with his healthcare providers. They regularly reach out to Mike; they get him engaged. They give him appointment options that are conducive to his late night work. Because the care is connected and coordinated, they get Mike into a diabetes management program. Because of the data and the analytics, Mike never has kidney failure, and Mike never goes to the ER. Mike doesn't miss six weeks of work, and unlike Joe, who spent months combating kidney failure, Mike stays healthy and he doesn't miss important events with his family."

Explorys' Noble Sales Purpose is, *We unlock the power of BIG DATA to improve healthcare for everyone.* When I worked with their leadership team to create and roll out their NSP we used the above story as an example of patient impact. Explorys shares their purpose and this story in new hire orientations on day one. Mihalik says, "We spend a lot of time talking about our purpose. If you're developing algorithms, or writing code, or doing data quality assurance,

I want you to think about Joe and his quality of life. Think about the health of our 50 million patients, and the impact our data has on their families and their lives."

Being intentional about humanizing patients who might otherwise be simply data ignites more engagement and ultimately, innovation. Mihalik says, "We have developers and software engineers who could do this work anywhere, they could go anywhere to solve big problems. Why would they want to do it here, in Cleveland Ohio?" Explorys is intentional about creating a direct connection to the patient because they want every member of their team to understand the meaning behind their work. Mihalik says, "Our health is our greatest asset, but we tend to take for granted what it means to be healthy, until it's compromised. Whether it's a small compromise like the flu or a common cold, or a big compromise like a cancer diagnosis, once it happens, it puts you in check. You immediately realize how important it is." Explorys wants their team dialed into the realities of people whose lives they're improving. Mihalik says, "When you're sick even the simple things become difficult. Walking your kids to the school bus, or getting down on the floor to play with them, becomes compromised."

Keeping patients front and center isn't always natural for a tech company, but Explorys recognizes that it gives them multiple competitive advantages. Their people become more emotionally mature, their work has larger purpose, they're more innovative, and they're able to recruit more top talent. Explorys' revenue has grown exponentially. In 2015, they were acquired by IBM to become part of IBM's new Watson Health unit. The Explorys leadership team, who created their purpose, is now scaling it in even bigger ways.

Finding noble purpose in healthcare doesn't seem like a big stretch. Yet many organizations leave it to chance. They assume that everyone cares about patients or the disease, or the cure. Most people in healthcare care passionately about patients. But in the rush of daily demands people can lose site of why the organization exists in the first place. Naming and claiming a purpose takes what is implicit, and makes it explicit. It enables you to operationalize your best intentions. Such is the case of F. Hoffman-LaRoche. This 120-year-old company's legacy is rooted in a patient-driven ethos, and they boldly proclaim their current purpose, ***Doing now what patients need next,*** in all of their documents.

The company was founded on October 1, 1896 by Fritz Hoffmann-La Roche. At the age of 28, Hoffman-La Roche was among the first to recognize that the industrial manufacture of medicines would be a major advance in the fight against disease. In the 120 years since, F. Hoffman-La Roche, Ltd., or Roche as they are more commonly referred to, has become the third-largest pharma company in the world. Based in Basel, Switzerland, their fiscal 2014 revenue was 47.46 billion Swiss francs, or approximately $48 billion US. Roche's Pharmaceuticals and Diagnostics Divisions supply products spanning the health care spectrum, from the early detection and prevention of disease to diagnosis and treatment.

Their purpose—*Doing now what patients need next*—is illustrated on their website with a video of their employees describing why they do the work that they do. I've worked with several Roche teams. I'm always impressed that wherever you go in the world, every single person at Roche knows their purpose statement. They not only know it, they live it in their daily jobs.

For example, Global Medical Scientific Liaison, Nathalie Schrameijer, MD, says, "Medical people are scientists; they're scientifically educated people talking to other scientifically educated people. We are talking about facts; it's talking about numbers. When you talk about drugs and study results, you have to talk about study results because it proves the drugs' efficacy."

As a physician herself, Dr. Schrameijer understands the need for accurate data. Yet, she says, "It's easy to lose yourself in those numbers, and forget what it actually means for the patients."

Schrameijer says, "If we only talk about that number, and not what improvement means to a patient, we're not as compelling. For a rheumatoid arthritis patient, a 10 percent improvement could be the difference of being able to open your prescription bottle. It might mean being able to use your knife to cut your own meat at the dinner table with your family."

The dignity of being able to open your own pill bottle and cut your own meat means the ability to remain an adult with your family versus becoming a patient. Schrameijer says, "When we use language and stories like that, we become more memorable. For Roche, this is how our medical organization can be even more impactful."

Kevin Hewitt, a Roche International Product Manager, says, "We constantly ask how can we put the patient at the center?" During a recent launch meeting, Roche brought patients on stage to discuss how their lives had been changed by their treatments.

Hewitt said, "The reaction from 300 people was stunning. We weren't just saying, 'We need to do now what patients need next.' We were showing them exactly what it looked like in action."

Leaders at Roche have long understood the universal business truth I stated in the opening chapter: the internal story becomes the external story. As a Noble Purpose leader, your role is to help your team internalize the impact you can have on individual human beings, no matter what product your organization sells.

Dr. Schrameijer says, "My message [to my team] is 'If you really want to make a change for the patient, make sure in every conversation with a physician to communicate scientific data as if it is your own relative. Communicate it as if it is your own family member.'"

At this point, you may be thinking, that's all fine and well for people who save lives, but my business isn't quite as dramatic. Even leaders in less sexy businesses can humanize their customers.

Making Basements Meaningful

Foundation Supportworks is a family-owned business based in Omaha, Nebraska. They manufacture state-of-the-art foundation repair and stabilization products to repair settling, bowing, cracked, and damaged foundations in residential, commercial, and municipal structures.

They were originally founded in 1975 as Thrasher Basements Systems, a one-man waterproofing company started by Greg Thrasher when he was just 20 years old. He says that back then, "I was a kid with a sledgehammer and a truck." Growing up he'd always assumed he would one day take over his father's grain elevator, but then his father sold it. After graduating from high school, Thrasher says, "I didn't have anything to do, so I went to Iowa where my uncle had a waterproofing business. I spent a week with him. I came back, got a pickup, and a sledgehammer, and started a waterproofing company. His wife Nancy, who was his girlfriend back then, says, "I was in high school. We lived in a small town in Iowa. Dave told me he was going to get business cards. I had never even known anyone who had a business card."

The Thrashers ran the business out of their home for 20 years. Nancy did the books, ran the office, and took phone calls. She says, "It wasn't like the phone was ringing off the hook in the beginning." As the business began to grow, they moved to Omaha, for more opportunity. They added people, but they still ran it from their house. Nancy says, "At one point we had three full-time people working in our basement." When revenue moved north of the $3 million mark, they moved into commercial facilities.

Today, Foundation Supportworks is a $100 million dollar company with 265 employees. They're the leading manufacturer of foundation repair and stabilization products. If your basement is leaking or the foundation of your home or commercial property is caving in, they can fix it. Or as they like to say, they not only fix it, they "fix it forever." They have a network of independently owned foundation repair contractors that spans the United States and Canada.

Greg Thrasher says, "As that 20-year-old kid, never in my wildest dreams would I have imagined this." The company scaled slowly at first, but then rapidly when Greg and Nancy realized the potential. Their children eventually joined the business. Dave, the younger brother, is president of Foundation Supportworks. His older brother Dan is president of Thrasher, Inc. Foundation Supportworks manufactures patented foundation products and Thrasher is their largest dealer. Thrasher and their other dealers across North America sell and install Foundation Supportworks products in homes and commercial spaces.

Dave and Dan grew up hearing their mother and father on the phone, taking care of customers. Nancy says, "Our kids heard Greg on the phone and his enthusiasm for customers." When they were as young as 14, both boys went on job sites with their dad. They got down into dirty basements and did the tough work needed to make things right for the customer." Greg Thrasher says he learned customer care from his father. "It was something I grew up with. Working with my dad, it was a customer-based business." He says, "I learned how to treat customers. The only way I could grow my business was to do it right the first time."

Working in basements isn't glamorous. Their team goes into crawlspaces to shore up floors. They dig through rocks and dirt to install retaining systems. They vacuum up dirty water. They clean up after mold. It's hard work. Their customers aren't always glamorous either. They're often middle-income families, for whom a leaking basement can be a financial crisis.

The Thrashers are intentional about humanizing their customers. Greg Thrasher says, "In every meeting we talk about how important our customers are and the problems they're having. These aren't fun problems to have. It's not like going to a furniture store and buying a new living room. This is the last thing people want to spend money on. We empathize with our customers, and we seed that with our employees."

Thrasher tells his team, "You go out there and people whose homes are falling apart, they are not going to be the happiest people in the world."

Painting an empathetic picture of customers helps the foundation support team see the intrinsic value of their work. Director of Sales Development Kurtis Kammerer, says, "Here we are just a bunch of construction guys out there fixing people's houses. But when you look at the impact you have on their house, and their family, and the community, it's huge."

I confess, I've always had a soft spot in my heart for people who do tough dirty jobs. Whenever I see a paving crew on the highway, or a guy leaning out of a bucket truck 50 feet in the air, or roofers banging it out on a sweltering day, I'm grateful. People like that fix and build stuff so the rest of us don't have to worry about it. It's physically demanding, and takes more brains than most people realize.

The leaders at Foundation Supportworks feel the same way. Vice President of Strategy Amanda Harrington, says "When I see pictures of Dave and Dan Thrasher as skinny teenagers in their muscle T-shirts working on a crew, it's part of our heritage. I love hearing those stories over and over again."

Sales Development Director Kammerer helps connect the dots between hard physical work and the impact on customers. He says, "I tell people, 'That customer, that's your grandmother. That person with the falling-down house, who is worried about the money it will cost to fix it, that person is just like your grandmother. Our job is to keep them safe. To help them retain the value of their biggest asset [their home].'"

The Foundation Supportworks belief—*Fix it now, and fix it forever*—stems from their commitment to their customers. Their leaders have driven exponential sales growth, and created the strongest dealer network in North America because they were purposeful about bringing the customers to life in the hearts and minds of every single one of their employees and dealers. For them, every customer is someone's grandmother.

Customer Impact is the Ultimate End Game

Explorys could have limited their focus to data accuracy. Roche could have simply touted drug efficacy. Foundation Supportworks could have treated their workers the way most construction companies do—just provide technical training and send them to the job site.

But the leaders in these organizations went further. They were intentional about humanizing the very real people they were serving.

Bringing the customers to life in vivid ways sparks greater engagement, connection, and, innovation. Not humanizing the customers puts you at risk. It's the death of emotional engagement. Customers wind up becoming a benign abstraction, or even an intrusion.

My father used to tell a classic story from when he was the branch manager for a bank. He overhead two tellers discussing their jobs in the break room; one said, "This job would be pretty good if it weren't for all the customers." The other agreed, "Customers really are a pain."

At this point, the top of my father's head exploded. You've probably experienced a similar lack of customer awareness in your own organization, or with a supplier.

A negative perception of customers is not uncommon. How many times have you been in a store or restaurant where an employee clearly indicated they were not pleased to have you there?

Lack of customer understanding and negative perceptions of customers spring from the same place. They occur when leaders don't paint a vivid, fully human picture of customers. As Edward Deming said, "If the majority of people behave in a particular way the majority of the time, the problem is not the people, the problem is the system." In top-performing organizations, people are rooting for their customers. They feel an emotional connection to customers because their leaders have been intentional about keeping them front and center every day.

Melissa Reiff is president of The Container Store, the chain based in Coppell, Texas, which introduced mainstream organization and made it cool. She talks to her team about the impact their products have on customers. "Even if you're the most disorganized person in the world, if you just organize your junk drawer you feel great. There is some kind of amazing gratification, in this chaotic world we live in, if you just organize your junk."

Organizations that adopt customer-centric cultures for the sake of improving service ratings often create cultures where their people feel as though they've become indentured servants to the customers. It's a reactionary approach. At The Container Store, the team is focused on customers because they want to improve their lives. Reiff says, "Our purpose is to continue to give this gracious gift of organization to our customers, and create an organized life for them."

Consumers consistently rate The Container Store as a top retail establishment. In their first year, employees receive 263 hours of formal training, compared to the industry average of 8 hours. The Container Store is a regular on *Fortune* magazine's annual list of the 100 best places to work. Their people care about your junk drawer.

Humanizing customers is about giving your team an empathetic vision of individual customers, which empowers them to be proactive on the customers' behalf. Customers don't dictate your strategy or your operation. In Noble Purpose organizations, strategy and operations are rooted in your deep understanding of customers, and your ingenuity about what's possible for them. Humanizing your customers makes your own job more fun, and your team more effective.

6

Dare to Be Different

Whenever you find yourself on the side of majority, it is time to pause and reflect

—Mark Twain

For many people, the Toronto-based travel company, G Adventures is the go-to team for experiencing the world. G (as they refer to themselves) offers more than 1,000 small-group experiences, safaris, and expeditions on all seven continents, to more than 100,000 travelers a year. From African safaris and Asian cultural treks to Italian family vacations and Eastern exotic expeditions, G creates adventures that are meaningful and memorable. They've won multiple awards. National Geographic Adventures named them as the best "Do It All Outfitter" on Earth. They're among the Top 100 Employers and 50 Best Managed Companies in Canada. Founder Bruce Poon Tip has been named an Ernst & Young EY Entrepreneur of the Year—twice.

Of course, it wasn't always this way. Poon Tip started the company after returning from a backpacking tour of Asia in 1990. He was driven to share with others his passion and vision about experiencing adventures in an authentic and sustainable manner. He didn't have any funding, but that didn't stop him. He maxed out two personal credit cards, and G Adventures was born. What started off as a one-man show has grown to become the world's largest adventure travel company with over 1,350 employees.

When I first met Bruce in 2008, G Adventures was on the rise. By the time we started working together in 2011, G Adventures was a global force that had been growing at a rate of 25 percent per year.

To call the G Adventures employees True Believers is an understatement. Imagine a crazy band of multi-ethnicity, multi-age, blue jean-wearing, backpack-carrying individuals who are so passionate about their company that they spend their free time making music videos about their tours. Now crank up the volume six notches, add a few tattoos, throw in company values that include **Embrace the Bizarre** and **We Love Changing People's Lives** and you start to get an inkling about G Adventures' culture.

G Adventures has become the global leader because their people are on fire for changing the world through travel. "Our competitors are huge holding companies," says Poon Tip, "I knew that I wasn't going to be able to outspend them. One of the things we *could* do was create a connection with our customers that transcended what we do. It wasn't just about travel; it was about creating a purpose that didn't exist, that other companies couldn't duplicate no matter how much money they threw at it."

On G tours people get off the beaten path. They don't ride in big buses or stay in chain hotels. Instead, G uses local guides, often putting people in smaller vehicles or local trains. Travelers stay in locally owned hotels and inns. Money goes back into local economies. Whether it's cooking classes in Italy, spear fishing with the Aborigines in Australia, or hiking the Inca trail, from the higher end Comfort Trips to the Yolo backpack trips, G Adventures travelers encounter new horizons that open their minds and hearts. The G Adventures CEOs (Chief Experience Officers) share G's company values with travelers at the first trip dinner.

I've never met people more passionate about travelers. Yet when their team initially talked about travel agents, they became noticeably less enthusiastic. Half of G Adventures' business is sold directly to consumers; the other half of their business is sold through travel agents, who recommend them to clients. When we began working together, the G Adventures team was frustrated because many of their travel agent clients didn't seem to understand why G Adventures was different. One person said, "To many of the agents, we're just another tour company."

Igniting Passion in Resellers

We decided to do something radical. I challenged them, what if, instead of trying to sell the agents on how the tours created happiness for the travelers, the team focused on creating happiness for the travel agents?

For context, consider the life of a travel agent. Young people often become travel agents because they love to travel. In the early years of their careers, they enjoy the perks of supplier-sponsored travel. But as they get older with more responsibilities at work and home, they travel less. They spend their days at a desk booking fabulous trips for other people.

Now imagine a young enthusiastic G Adventures representative walking in saying, "Let's send your clients on these amazing trips that will change their lives!" The tours are amazing, but from the travel agent's perspective, the sales interaction is nondifferentiated. The travel agent is still staring at a water cooler. How could we create a differentiated experience for the agent?

We started with the big three discovery questions:

1. How do you make a difference?
2. How do you do it differently from your competition?
3. On your best day, what do you love about your job?

The "aha" moment came when one of the sales leaders said, "I wish the travel agents felt the same sense of purpose that we do."

We decided that if G Adventures was serious about changing lives, they had to apply that same thinking to the agents. Using the three discovery questions, we settled on their NSP:

We help people discover more passion, purpose, and happiness.

With a bold NSP in place, our next challenge was to figure out how to help agents discover passion, purpose, and happiness, while sitting at their desks. And being G Adventures, we had to do it in a big, bold, quirky, fun way.

The first thing we did was rebrand the outside sales team. They became Global Purpose Specialists, or GPSs for short. Their new jobs weren't just to sell life-changing trips for consumers; they were to reignite the spark of passion in travel agents.

We launched the new strategy at a big travel conference. The G team had 7 minutes to present their offerings in front of hundreds of travel agents. They were wedged in between 20 competitors who were doing the usual dog and pony "here's how wonderful we are" presentations.

The G team took a different approach. The sales director kicked off their seven minutes by asking the auditorium of agents, "How many of you have ever booked a trip that made a difference in someone's life?" Almost every agent raised a hand. He then said, "Instead of talking about us, I'd like to spend this time talking about you. Please turn to the person next to you, and for the next two minutes describe who you booked that life-changing trip for and how it affected them. Then give the other person two minutes to do the same."

Keep in mind, the G team only had 7 minutes in front of this highly coveted group of resellers. Now they've given away over half their time letting them talk among themselves. Here's what happened: the room came alive. Five minutes earlier they had been jaded travel agents listening to endless pitches from cruise lines and hotels. Now they were animated, describing how they'd sent people on a Golden Anniversary at the Eiffel Tower, an *I survived cancer* trek through Scotland, or an *I found my true love at 60* Bali honeymoon. The energy in the room rose exponentially.

Because of the brain-science training we'd done, the G team knew that asking the agents to describe how they made a difference to someone would ignite their frontal lobes. Your frontal lobes are the control panel for your brain. It's where empathy and compassion sit. It's also where problem solving and creativity reside. Brain science research reveals that compassionate thoughts light up the frontal lobe of a person's brain. The frontal lobe is where the mind can access solutions. As soon as we begin to experience compassionate thoughts, this part of the brain lights up, and we can literally go from "impossible" to "possible" in an instant.[1]

With that single question—How many of you have ever booked a trip that made a difference in someone's life?—the G team put the agents in a totally different mental space. Instead of passively taking in information, as they did during the competitors' presentations, the agents became actively engaged. By asking the agents to describe their own experiences, the G team reignited the agents' pride and passion. In that moment, the agents became the best versions of themselves.

This is a critical point. Living your purpose means more than pitching your company in an inspirational way. Companies with purpose add value to customers in every customer interaction, even when they're not buying.

Let's go back to the auditorium. With two minutes left of their allotted seven minutes, the G team called the room back to order. The sales director, who at that point hadn't even introduced himself yet said, "The way you feel right now, is the way we want you to feel every single day."

He went on, "Your job changes peoples lives. You give people memories that last a lifetime. Sometimes in the hustle of business, it's easy for you to forget just how much you matter in the lives of your customers. We want to make sure that doesn't happen. We have a team of Global Purpose Specialists. Our job is to help you discover more passion, purpose, and happiness in your job, and in

---

[1] Mary Robinson, "The Power of Compassion," *Lifelines to Laughlines* blog.

your life. Our team has been trained to make you feel like this every time you interact with us."

He closed saying, "Here's a video to remind you that you're part of an amazing industry. My name is Ron Fenska, and if you'd like to talk to us about passion, purpose, and happiness, come meet us at our booth."

And with that he walked off the stage as a music video played, showing G Adventures employees in exotic spots all over the world lip-syncing to "Find Me Somebody to Love." (Watch the video on Vimeo; it's inspiring.)

That afternoon, the G Adventures booth was swamped. They had to run back to the van for more brochures. They lined up sales calls for weeks to come. Are you surprised that event leaders asked them to speak at future events?

After the big splash, the next step was to bring their purpose to life during individual agent interactions. For this, we created the Purpose Cards. The size of a standard deck of cards, they're G Adventures branded cards printed with different, quirky questions, like What's the most beautiful sunset you've ever seen while traveling? Or, Why did you get into the travel industry?

The GPS team uses them with agents. When they're scheduling a sales call, the GPS says to the agent, "I've got something new, it's a tool to help you love your job more. It's more fun if we do it with other people. Can you get the rest of the agents in the office together for me to show you?"

They start the group meeting by having the agents pick a card from the deck. Then they talk about their answers. They become engaged; they inevitably want to ask more questions from more cards. Agents ask for a set of cards to use with their own clients. During the interaction, the GPS then segues to, "You'll love using these with clients. We use these cards on our trips, travelers love them." Then it's an easy natural conversation to talk about the trips. In fact, after being prompted by the cards, agents will often ask questions about what travelers experience on a G trip.

Think about what's happening here; instead of meeting with just one reseller, the GPS is meeting with an entire office. Instead of talking, they're listening as agents open their hearts about their own experiences with travel. Instead of leaving a brochure that will go in the circular file, the agents *ask* for a G Adventures branded sales tool to use with their own clients. Instead of pitching a product, the GPS is discussing products (tours) in the context of customer experiences. And at the end of the sales call, the agents often ask the GPS to come back to meet with more agents, and their boss.

When was the last time your team got that kind of reaction from a single sales call?

G Adventures changed the conversation with their customers. They didn't do it in a manipulative way; it was authentic. They truly wanted travel agents to experience the same passion they had. They created competitive differentiation and established greater leadership in the market. In the two years since they implemented the purpose-driven approach to agents, G Adventures revenue has grown 35 percent each year (versus their previous sustained 25 percent growth).

Here's what we can learn from G's success:

1. **Establish a clear NSP.**

   Passion, purpose, and happiness aren't just warm fuzzies to the team at G. It's something leaders expect their teams to bring to life with customers.

2. **Pay attention to the person in front of you.**

   Many organizations view resellers as nothing more than a route to the customer, and oftentimes they're seen as an unwelcome obstacle. I've heard resellers described as everything from a necessary evil to partners with whom we need to "win mind share." Those approaches tend to create an environment focused on the company of origin and commissions rather than the reseller experience. G Adventures decided that the agents were more than mere resellers. They were real live human beings who deserved to love their jobs. They made resellers their end game, instead of treating them as a vehicle to get to someone better.

3. **Deliver value whether people buy or not.**

Agents don't have to buy from G to have a G experience. G is intentional about bringing their purpose to life in every interaction with a customer or prospective customers. Their purpose isn't simply to sell people; it's to help change their lives. Because of their authenticity, their reputation is widespread. Customers are eager to meet with them, which naturally translates into more sales.

4. **Don't be afraid to do something different.**

Professional doesn't have to mean boring. But, sadly, it usually does. How many endless 26-point presentations do we have to sit through before leaders realize the following: Logic makes you think, but emotion makes you *act*. The purpose cards and the reframe on group presentations weren't designed to showcase new features. They were designed to create a more authentic emotional connection. Later, when I suggested creating a big purple bag of games and tricks (sorry, contents confidential) to use on sales calls, no one worried that it would be unprofessional. Instead, the GPS team jumped in with ideas to fill it.

Igniting passion isn't the unique purview of businesses like software, pharmaceuticals, or travel. If the team at Foundation Support Works can ignite passion for leaky basements, you can find the noble cause in your own business. Don't let being part of a less glamorous business, or running a smaller company, hold you back.

Later in the book you'll meet Porter Keadle Moore, an Atlanta-based accounting firm whose NSP is *We help clients seize opportunity and reduce risk*. You'll also meet Thompson Dehydrating, a Topeka, Kansas manufacturing firm who works with renewable fuels and biomass. Their NSP is *We make the world, and our customers, cleaner, safer, and more prosperous*.

Living your NSP requires mindfulness. It requires purity of attention for the person in front of you. The team at G Adventures thought long and hard about how they could make life better for travel agents. They're intentional about the emotional under-pinnings of their interactions.

Too often, organizations treat resellers, recommenders, and sometimes even customers, as transactions to get somewhere better. I've seen entire sales courses devoted to "Getting past the Gatekeeper." You certainly want your people to set priorities based on where they can provide the most mutual value, for customers and for you.

Leaders must recognize, though, that every person in your organization is creating your reputation. And so is every person they interact with. When people aren't fully attentive to the person in front of them, they miss opportunities to live your purpose.

Every business has meaning. The challenge for you, the leader, is to give it ample airtime.

7

Be Brutal about Airtime

The successful warrior is the average man, with laser-like focus.
—Bruce Lee

How would you evaluate your airtime?

You might be surprised at how your people perceive you. After I wrote *Selling with Noble Purpose*, readers started emailing me about problems they were experiencing with their bosses. Many of those emails sounded similar:

Dear Lisa,

I'm a top performer at XYZ company. I'm always in the President's Club, Gold Level Circle, etc. Selling with Noble Purpose describes what I've always believed about business. You put into words what I try to do with my customers. I want to improve their lives. That's why I'm the number one salesperson (customer service rep, operations guy, etc.).

"But . . ."

Can you guess what comes next?

My boss (CEO, VP, etc.) doesn't care about this stuff. All they care about is money.

I got some version of this message at least once a week, and have for the past two years. It's a heartfelt missive from a top performer who cares deeply about customers, yet is disheartened because they think all their boss cares about is money.

When I first started getting these emails, I was at a loss for a reply. Were all these top performers right? Were their leaders really driven *solely* by quarterly earnings and their own bonuses? Was there even an inkling of customer care inside them?

I didn't want to ignore the problem. I decided it was time to take to heart our own NSP, *We help leaders drive revenue and do work that makes them proud.*

I emailed the top performers, saying "Thanks for your note. I tell you what, send me your VP's or CEO's address and I'll send them a copy of *Selling with Noble Purpose*, on me."

That's when it started to get weird. I began to hear from the leaders. Their emails went something like this:

Dear Lisa,

Thanks for the *Noble Purpose* book. This is exactly what I have always believed about business, it's all about the customer.

But . . .

Can you guess what comes next?

I can't get the people who work for me to understand. All they care about are their paychecks.

At first, I assumed this was small-scale cognitive dissonance. A few leaders saying the right words, but believing and acting very differently. When I kept getting the same emails over and over, I realized, this is a more widespread problem.

The front-line people believe that their business is all about the customer.

The senior leaders believe that their business is all about the customer.

Yet neither believes that the other truly cares about customers. Why the disconnect?

I thought about it for weeks, turning it over and over in my mind. It became like a chemistry experiment, where you're breaking down compounds looking for the element that is causing the reaction. It felt complex; then I remembered a situation I encountered with a kindergarten classroom. Suddenly I realized, maybe this isn't as hard as I'm making it out to be.

When my youngest daughter was in kindergarten, I regularly volunteered in her classroom. One day, the kids were making Mother's Day presents. The teacher asked the kids, "What are your mother's favorite things to do? The kids then wrote and drew examples of the activities their moms loved best. My job was to staple their pages together into booklets, as gifts for their mothers.

Naturally, I read them.

I was stunned. According to an entire classroom of five- and six year olds, the two things most of their mothers love best are cleaning and sleeping. Clearly, this merited further investigation. I asked a few of the kids, "How do you know your mommy loves to clean and sleep so much?"

Their answers?

"She talks about it all the time. She's always saying we have to clean up around here." If she's not talking about cleaning, she's talking about how tired she is. One kindergartener, whose parents also had a baby and a toddler at home, performed an imitation of his mother, head in her hand, saying, "*I am sooo tired. I have got to get some sleep.*"

Cleaning and sleeping were what their mothers talked about the most often. The kids naturally assumed those two activities were the most important things to their mothers.

The words of the leader matter.

Whatever subject you give the most airtime to will be what people assume is most important to you. The same thing happens in organizations. Wherever leaders spend their airtime is going to be what people presume to be most important to those leaders.

The reason so many people believe their leaders only care about money is because that's what leaders devote their airtime to. At this stage, you may be thinking, *That's right, that's all my boss or board focus on, money.* That may be true.

But before we talk about your boss or board, let's get brutally honest about you. If someone evaluated your airtime, what would they think is most important to you?

People don't always give ample airtime to the things they care about most. Think about the mothers of those kindergartners. Most of them would probably be quite disheartened to discover that their children believe that cleaning and sleeping are their favorite activities. Yet, the kids reached a completely logical conclusion, based on what they heard.

People don't know what's in your heart, unless you tell them.

In our consulting practice, we evaluate an organization's airtime. We observe meetings, internal communications, and senior leadership interactions. More often than not, leaders are stunned to discover how little time they spend talking about customer impact as opposed to internal metrics.

Positioning expert Mark Levy says, "The amount of real estate you devote to an idea tells people what is important."

Look over your company's annual report. Read your presentations. Read your marketing materials. Read your emails.

If you were an outsider looking at these documents, what conclusions would you reach about your organization? What about your interactions with your team? The amount of airtime you give a topic in a meeting tells people what's important. The amount of time you spend on a topic in a speech tells people what you care about.

Earlier in the book, I talked about lagging versus leading indicators. Profit and productivity are lagging indicators. Leader airtime in meetings is a leading indicator, and so is the language in marketing and sales aids, and customer presence in team interactions. These indicators aren't as easy to measure as revenue, but they can be evaluated. One technique we use is a Wordle. We take an organization's marketing and sales aids, or website copy, or the notes from a large meeting, and feed it into a Wordle program. The program produces a word cloud, which is an image of words that were used in your document or meeting. The size of each word in the word cloud indicates its frequency of use. The most frequently used words show up as the largest words. Lesser-used words are smaller. It's a visual representation of how you're spending your airtime. Leaders are usually stunned by the results. Meeting notes are the real killer. When a leader sees a word cloud produced from the transcript of his or her meeting with the words *profit*, *revenue*, and *earnings* in 48-point type and the word *customer* barely visible in 10-point type, there's no denying how that leader is spending his or her airtime.

You remember Blackbaud, the Charleston, South Carolina, cloud company from Chapter 1. Figure 7.1 is a Wordle we created from Blackbaud's sales presentations before they became intentional about their purpose.

The large words reflect where they were spending the majority of their airtime. Notice, the majority of these words are product-focused (*Raiser Edge and module* refer to their software) or company-focused (Blackbaud). Figure 7.2 is a Wordle created from some of their more recent materials.

Notice how the larger words in this Wordle are customer-impact focused. Blackbaud is now talking about what matters

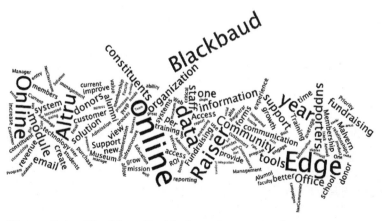

Figure 7.1   Blackbaud's Airtime Pre-Purpose

Figure 7.2   Blackbaud's Airtime Post-Purpose

to their customers (*giving, participating, time*) and how to make a difference this year. Blackbaud's organizational airtime, both inside and outside the organization, is about customer-impact.

Becoming a Noble Purpose Leader requires that you be intentional about your airtime. If you want your team to understand that you have a bigger purpose than money, you must give ample airtime to your aspirations.

The mothers of the kindergarteners made the most classic airtime error. They gave more airtime to seemingly urgent issues than they did to important ones. I've made the same mistake myself, both with my family and in my career. Most leaders struggle with this issue. Perhaps you're familiar with Stephen Covey's important versus urgent grid, shown in Figure 7.3.

In the crush of daily operations, what may seem urgent is not actually necessarily the most important. The highest impact items—like strategy and planning—rarely seem urgent, yet they are of great importance. The challenge with purpose is that even when leaders recognize its importance it rarely feels urgent. In fact, it almost never feels urgent. Mediocre leaders don't give purpose proper airtime because the urgent demands of daily business take precedence.

Yet your team is drawing conclusions about the impact of their work every single day. Their belief about their work *is*

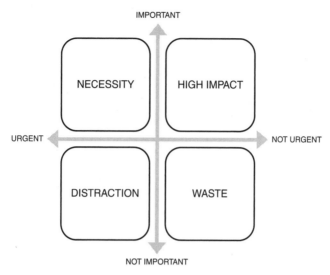

Figure 7.3

an urgent matter. As their leader, you play a powerful role in determining how they interpret their jobs. A November 2, 2015 *Fast Company* article, entitled **The Purpose-Driven Workforce Is 42 Million Strong**,[1] cited a survey of 6,332 adults that revealed that only 28 percent of the workforce is purpose-oriented. The article documents that purpose-oriented employees do better work, have higher well-being, stay in their jobs for longer, and are better ambassadors for their employers. As a leader, you have a strong incentive to set the right tone.

Your words tell your team whether their work is meaningful, or whether they're merely expendable assets in the service of making money. If you're the CEO, you already know how powerful your words are. People repeat your words to each other every single day. The same can be said of individual managers, perhaps even more so. Studies show that the words of an individual manager have dramatic impact on how people perceive their jobs, and their company.

---

[1]Ben Schiller, "The Purpose-Driven Workforce Is 42 Million Strong," *Fast Company*, November 2, 2015.

A KPMG survey of their employees found that employees whose managers talked about KPMG's impact on society were 42.4 percent more likely to describe the firm as a great place to work.[2] Of those with managers who talked up meaning, 68 percent indicated they rarely think about looking for new jobs outside KPMG; that fell to 38 percent for employees whose managers didn't discuss meaning.

Think about that for a minute. These people work for the exact same company. They do the exact same jobs. People whose managers don't talk about meaning are almost twice as likely to think about looking for other jobs. Proving yet again:

The Words of the Leader Matter

Losing people costs time and money. Author and consultant Scott Wintrip, who created the concept of On-Demand Hiring, works with organizations like Randstad, Boeing, and Procter & Gamble. Wintrip says, "An empty seat usually takes more than 25 work days to fill, draining profitability an average of $23,000 every time it happens." That's only the hard costs; the costs to morale and customer retention is even greater. Even if people are only *thinking* about looking for another job, as they were in the KMPG situation, it's still mental distraction. They're not all in for their current jobs because they're constantly thinking about better opportunities.

If you had a tool that would double the likelihood of retaining your best people, and keeping them focused, you would use it every day. You have such a tool. It's your airtime.

As a Noble Purpose leader, you must be brutally honest with yourself about how you're spending your own airtime. We'll talk about your boss in a minute.

---

[2]Rachel Feintzeig, "I Don't Have a Job. I Have a Higher Calling," *Wall Street Journal*, February 24, 2015.

First, let's get an accurate assessment on how you're doing. Try this exercise over the course of the next week: observe your interactions with your team. Make a note of what you spend the most time talking about. Are you talking about product features or customer impact? Are you talking about internal metrics or customer success? Are you talking about customers as aggregates or individuals?

People are usually surprised to see where they're spending their largest volume of words. If you're disappointed in your own assessment, don't be too hard on yourself. Many leaders care deeply about customers, but up until this point, there hasn't been a clear language to express it. As we've seen, the money story is the default narrative of business. It's challenging to keep purpose at the forefront of our conversations. It takes time to talk about meaning. A spreadsheet can be forwarded; an email describing customer impact is going to take a few minutes to write. As people get overloaded, narrative gets pushed to the back burner.

As an individual leader, moving from a money story to a meaning story requires that you be intentional. Knowing that your words have a dramatic and lasting impact, think about what you want to bring forth with your team.

Mediocre leaders often view purpose as something they'll get to when they have time (Figure 7.4). This is another way of saying that it's neither urgent nor important.

Noble purpose leaders know that giving more to meaning and purpose is important (Figure 7.5). They make time for it, and they give it appropriate airtime in daily operations.

As a leader, when you decide to give your purpose more airtime, you can make the change quickly. It takes work, and old habits are hard to break, but it's 100 percent within your control. Now that you know that shifting your airtime will make you twice as likely to keep your best people, you have an immediate incentive.

Shifting your organization's airtime is challenging, but it's also doable.

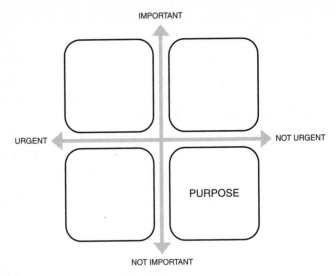

Figure 7.4   Mediocre Leaders

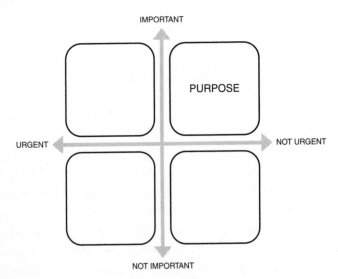

Figure 7.5   Noble Purpose Leaders

KPMG Global Chairman John Veihmeyer says, "We can see ourselves as bricklayers or cathedral builders."

If you want your organization to be perceived as cathedral builders, you need to talk like cathedral builders, and act like cathedral builders. In less successful organizations, cathedral building (meaning and purpose) is something HR talks about, or it shows up in the marketing materials. It might get a little airtime at the annual meeting, but it won't be the focus. When it's crunch time, which it is most days, it's all about laying the bricks. The fact that the bricks are contributing to a beautiful cathedral gets forgotten.

Are the demands of your operation going to be less pressing in the future? Is the need for financial results going to go away? Of course not. That's why you need a framework and a language for bringing purpose to the fore.

Think about group meetings in your organization; what gets talked about? Do leaders spend group time going over reports and details that could be just as easily sent by email? Or do they use the time to win hearts and minds?

One phenomenon I consistently observe is the Death by Power Point meeting. It's particularly problematic for organizations where the annual or quarterly meetings are the only time leaders have the opportunity to get in front of the field.

Here's how it usually plays out. It's time for the big meeting. You tell yourselves that this year it's going to be different. It's going to be fun. It's going to be inspiring. It will be action-oriented. Yet as the meeting gets closer, everyone wants to get on the agenda. Each department is eager to share their plans and updates. The product people want to talk about their new bells and whistles. Marketing wants to introduce the new campaign. Finance needs to share the numbers and so on. Leaders are so focused on the information they want to share that they forget about the feeling they're trying to evoke. The result is a ballroom full of people looking at endless slides packed with internal information in a 12-point font.

You can do better.

Airtime is more than just the words that you say; it's also the actions you take. It's where you put your emphasis. In our interview for this book, Wharton School professor Adam Grant, author of the bestseller *Give and Take,* said, "You reveal your priorities through what you do and not what you say, actions speak louder than words and actions speak more accurately than words."

If you start your meeting with a compelling customer-impact story but the rest of your airtime is devoted to internal metrics, your team will see your priorities. Grant, who is consistently ranked as one of the world's top business professors, says, "Core values are clear when there are trade-offs. What do the leaders do when there is a clear trade-off between serving customers and other agendas?"

Grant has researched what happens when leaders focus employees on the beneficiaries of their work. In a 2010 Wharton paper, Grant writes, "Employees who know how their work has a meaningful, positive impact on others are not just happier than those who don't; they are vastly more productive, too.

It's not touchy feely—Grant has documented his research, a series of research papers. The Wharton article says, "In one experiment, he [Grant] studied paid employees at a public university's call center, who were asked to phone potential donors to the school. It can be grim work: employees don't get paid much and suffer frequent rejections from people unhappy about getting calls during dinner. Turnover is high and morale is often low. So how do you motivate workers to stay on the phone and bring in the donations?

In his 2007 study, Grant and a team of researchers—Elizabeth Campbell, Grace Chen, David Lapedis, and Keenan Cottone from the University of Michigan—arranged for one group of call center workers to interact with scholarship students who were the recipients of the school's fundraising largess. It wasn't a long meeting—just a five-minute session where the workers were able to ask each student about his or her studies. But over the next month, that little chat made a big difference. The call center was able to monitor both the amount of time its employees spent on the phone and the amount of donation dollars they brought in. A month later, callers who had interacted with the scholarship students spent more than two times as many minutes on the phone, and brought in vastly more money: a weekly average of $503.22, up from $185.94."

The researchers concluded, in their paper titled, "Impact and the Art of Motivation Maintenance: The Effects of Contact with Beneficiaries on Persistence Behavior," the following: "Even minimal, brief contact with beneficiaries can enable employees to maintain their motivation."

Your airtime is a combination of your words and actions. It's your opportunity to help your team understand who the beneficiaries of their work are, and how they affect them. Earlier in the book we talked about being intentional, and mindfulness. Nowhere are these practices more important than when the leader addresses your team. If you're leading a group meeting or you're sending organizational correspondence, here are some questions to ask of yourself and your team, to help you be intentional about giving your purpose adequate airtime:

- How do we want people to feel as a result of this meeting or communication?
- What would our people find the most meaningful?
- How do we want our people to perceive our organization?
- What do we want our people to care about?
- What do we want our people to know about our customers?
- What do we want our leaders to communicate to their teams?
- How do we want our customer-facing people to talk to customers?
- What data is just as easily communicated via hand-outs or email?
- What information requires a story and an emotional connection?

These questions will help you and the other leaders in your organization get the best impact from your public airtime.

We've talked about you, we've talked about your organization, now let's talk about your boss. If you reread the email correspondence I shared in the opening of this chapter, it's tempting to think that the bosses who wrote me were only giving lip service to purpose. As observers, the employees are probably more accurate in assessing the bosses' airtime than the bosses themselves.

But I can tell you, after personally meeting many of the leaders whose employees wrote me, the bosses who primarily focus on money aren't bad people. Just like the moms of the kindergarteners who talk about cleaning and sleeping, they're well-intentioned human beings who are trying to do the best they can with the most pressing issues in front of them.

If you're frustrated with how your boss is spending his or her airtime, don't assume bad intent. As a leader, this is an opportunity for you to manage up, even if your boss is the CEO. My father once told me, "It doesn't matter what role you have, a big part of your job description is to make your boss successful." Your boss is just as busy, if not busier than you are. He or she may be facing all kinds of pressure you don't even know about. Good leaders have their bosses' back. You can use your personal airtime with your boss to shift the tone. The next time you meet with your boss say, "Before we get to the numbers, I'd like to talk about what they mean." Share a short customer-impact story. Tell your boss, "This is what drives me and my team to go the extra mile." Then wait for your boss to respond. More than likely you'll have a more strategic conversation. You'll put the wheels in motion to shift the organizational airtime.

If you have a good relationship with your boss, be straightforward. Share this book with him or her and say, "This will help our people be more effective." Assume good intent on the part of your bosses; they want your organization to be successful just as much as you do. If they haven't been talking about anything other than money or metrics, it may simply be because they didn't have the language to do so. As a Noble Purpose leader, your job is to help all the boats around you rise. Even your boss.

The Container Store President Melissa Reiff says, "The older I get and the more experience I get, the more I realize it's not simple to communicate in a way that makes people feel safe, secure, and warm."

When you become more intentional about giving your purpose airtime, conversations about product, promotion, processes, people, and so forth become more effective. In the next chapter, I'll introduce you to the 6-P model. It's a way to measure goals and accomplishments against your purpose.

Before we get into the model, let me share a very personal example to demonstrate how the lens of Noble Purpose will shift your airtime and make you better at the things you're already doing well.

My husband and I have been parents for over two decades. We have two daughters. We haven't been perfect parents, any more than either of our own parents, or any other parent is perfect.

Like many people, we looked for tips and techniques to help us be better parents. Early in our parenting journey we encountered research about how successful families, those who raise happy, well-adjusted, productive children, have dinner together several times a week.

Striving to have dinner together four nights a week is a great goal for any parent. If you're the kind of person who likes goals, you can even create a spreadsheet to chart your progress. Creating a target, in this instance four dinners a week, and implementing the tactics to make it happen, will have a positive effect on your family. It's a worthy endeavor for someone who wants to be a good parent.

But let's be honest, most people want to be more than just a *good* parent; if we're honest, most of us will admit that we aspire to be great parents. I know that's what I want. For my husband and I, parenting is a noble endeavor. It's our best opportunity to improve the arc of human history.

We believe that our purpose as parents is not just to raise happy children, but to raise future leaders who will make a difference in the world. It might sound hokey, or overly aspirational, but for us it's real. Raising future leaders is the purpose that has guided us through the long, sometimes boring, sometimes thrilling, often exhausting 20-year slog that is parenting.

With our purpose as our North Star, that same goal, four dinners a week, becomes more strategic. Now it's not just the quantity of the dinners; it's quality. If we want to raise leaders, we need to do more than just eat. We need to be intentional about how we're spending our airtime. A family dinner is better than no dinner at all. But a dinner where we talk about big issues, where we share ideas about how to make challenging decisions, where we ask our daughters their opinions about world events, where we talk about the meaning of love and friendship and world peace, that, my friends, is a very different dinner. That is not just a dinner; it's a dinner with Noble Purpose.

The lens of purpose—to raise future leaders—informs our airtime. We're more intentional about our conversations. We're also more inclined to meet our goal of four dinners, because now it's not just a tactic; it's critical to achieving our purpose. It's both urgent and important.

We're hardly perfect. Sometimes it's delivery pizza with no meaningful dialogue at all. Sometimes we've even fought at the table. But measuring ourselves against our purpose has made us more intentional about our airtime and has created a better environment than we would have otherwise had.

I often draw parallels between excellent leadership and excellent parenting. If you don't have children, think about your own parents. Whether they were intentional or not, they created a culture for your family. Their words shaped you, for better or worse, and in most cases, it was probably some of both.

Leadership is leadership, no matter what the arena. You don't have to be perfect to be excellent.

8

Create Your Purpose Framework

The uncreative mind can spot wrong answers, but it takes a very creative mind to spot wrong questions.
—Antony Jay, author of the British political comedies,
Yes Minister and *Yes, Prime Minister*

Good leaders look for accurate answers. Great leaders seek bigger questions. To create your purpose framework, you need to start asking different types of questions about your business.

In most organizations, the driving question is *how can we make more money off of our existing business model?* As we've seen in earlier chapters, this only sets you up for mediocrity. A better driving question is *how can we activate our NSP?*

Pointing your team in the direction of purpose doesn't mean that you don't track and measure money. Successful organizations are meticulous about money. As a Noble Purpose leader, you'll still track financial metrics, you'll just look at them through a different lens. As we've documented, looking through the lens of purpose will ultimately produce more money for you to track.

Purpose-focused organizations outperform profit-focused organizations because they ask better questions about the business. To illustrate, let's look at a typical business framework.

In every business, you have naturally competing interests. You need to produce exceptional products, but you have to keep them cost-effective for the customer and the market. You need efficient processes, but you can't sacrifice quality for efficiency. You want to hire, train, and retain top talent, but you can't let payroll or training budgets get out of line. You need unique promotions and marketing to capture market attention, but if you overspend, you won't recoup your investment.

We call these competing interests the 5-Ps (see Figure 8.1). A successful business has goals in each area.

Profit: financial goals and measurements
Process: internal productivity and quality standards
Products: innovation and development goals
Promotion: sales, marketing, and public relations goals and strategy
People: employee development metrics and goals

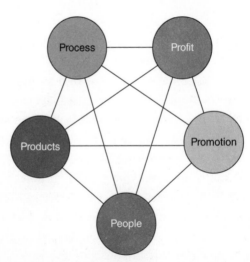

Figure 8.1   Traditional 5-P Model

There's a natural tension between each circle. When one pulls, the others feel a tug. Profit goals affect the goals for processes, products, promotion, and people. For example, if an organization is trying to improve profit margin, they may cut back on promotion or product development. They might put a halt to training and development (people). They may even sacrifice quality or short-circuit their processes.

A firm focused on process improvement might wind up reducing product quality or sacrificing morale (people) by enforcing unrealistic production mandates. Each circle affects the other circles. Overemphasizing goals in one area puts strain on the goals in other areas.

With no common purpose guiding the organization, people tend to treat their individual or departmental goals as organizational goals. This results in silos and turf wars. Each department clamors for their cause. There is no mutual alignment, and the consequences can be disastrous.

The most common, and ultimately fatal error is overemphasizing profit. As we've seen, it can be disastrous for morale and differentiation. Viewing the other functions through the lens of profit alone limits your thinking. When you primarily focus on profit, you're less likely to ask the kind of creative questions that could ultimately improve your value. Concentrating solely on profit removes your focus from the customer, stifles innovation, and distorts the entire system. It looks and feels like Figure 8.2.

Overemphasizing profits puts a strain on all of the others areas. In the short term they'll feel the strain. Over a longer period of time, these critical areas will suffer, and your business will be unsustainable.

When you overemphasize profit, you limit yourself to questions such as these:

- How can we make our processes faster and cheaper?
- Which products are the most profitable? How can we make them more profitable?

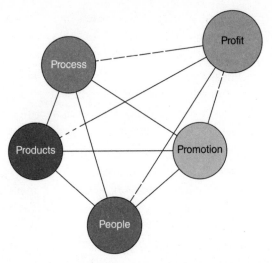

Figure 8.2   Overemphasis on Profit Puts Other Functions at Risk

- Which products are the least profitable? How can we change that?
- How much do our people cost? How can we generate more revenue with fewer people? How can we get each person to generate more revenue?
- What's our promotion expense? How do our sales and marketing costs compare with the industry? How can we cut them? How can we get sales to produce more revenue? How can we get them to reduce expenses?
- How can we make our people more efficient? What skills do they need to make us more profitable?

These are not bad questions. But they'll never ignite emotional engagement. Nor will they jumpstart innovation.

The new landscape of business calls for a different model. We've moved our clients from a traditional 5-P model to the Noble Purpose 6-P model (Figure 8.3). You'll notice that profit is not at the center of the 6-P model. Purpose is at the center. Profit is a measurement of how well you are performing against your Noble Sales

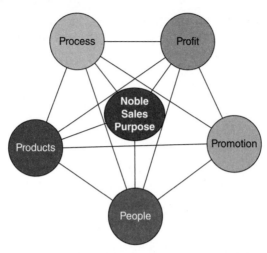

Figure 8.3   McLeod Noble Purpose 6-P Model

Purpose. Profit is one of the five key areas where you set goals and targets. However, it's not the center.

Having an NSP at the center prompts you to ask questions such as these:

- How do our processes affect our customers? How might we improve our processes to benefit our customers? How can we be more effective to better help our customers succeed?
- What are our customers' goals? What kinds of products would help them achieve those goals?
- How do our customers do business today? How might they do business in the future? How can we help them get there?
- What problems do our customers encounter? How can we help them solve these? What products, services, delivery systems, or programs can we create to address these issues?
- In what yet-to-be-imagined ways could we help our customers?
- How can our promotions reach more customers? How could we tailor our promotions to better serve our customers?
- How is our sales force helping our customers be more successful? How can our salespeople get better at that?

- What skills do our people need to make our customers more successful? What ideas do our people have for our customers?
- Are some customers more profitable than others? Why is that? Are we serving them better? If so, how can we duplicate that with other customers?
- Why are some customers less profitable? Are we doing too much or too little for those customers?

Can you see the difference?

The first set of questions—those centered on profits—is internally focused. They ask about your business: "How can we make more profit off what we're already doing now?" These type of questions view the other four Ps through the lens of profit alone. Those are the types of questions companies like Blockbuster asked when they were failing. They're focused on milking out as much money as possible from the existing model. Profit-focused questions blind you to changes in the market, and what your customers might want in the future. For example, profit-focused questions prompted Blockbuster to add candy at the checkout. Purpose-driven questions prompted Netflix to reinvent entertainment.

Purpose-driven questions are about improving the customer's condition. These are the type of questions companies like Flight Centre, Hootsuite, Roche, and Blackbaud ask. They promote innovation, and they create better organizational alignment. Instead of department goals, leaders are thinking about customer impact.

Look at the previous questions and think about your own team; which conversation are they going to find more interesting and engaging? Which set of questions is going to bring out their best thinking? Now think about your customers; which conversation do you think they would prefer you to be having?

Beautiful Questions versus Exhausting Questions

The poet and consultant Libby Wagner, who specializes in leadership language says, "There are beautiful questions and there are exhausting questions." Wagner draws upon the work of the late

Irish poet, John O'Donahue, and English poet, David Whyte, to describe the differences:

> A beautiful question by nature is expansive rather than restrictive. When you hear a beautiful question, it strikes a chord with you. It resonates. It can be both exciting and a little bit terrifying. It's big.
>
> An exhausting question is one that's the same question over and over again. Every time it comes up, You think, *Oh no, not this again.* It's restrictive. It keeps us in the same old conversations, week after week, year after year.

Wagner provides an example, "The question, *How are we going to increase sales?* can turn into a really exhausting question. Or, *How can we get the team to produce more?* A beautiful question is, *What would create an entirely different way of meeting the needs of our customers?*"

Beautiful questions give you energy. Exhausting questions deflate your energy. Wagner says, "A beautiful question is rooted ultimately in language."

Answering the second set of questions will help you create more nuanced, customer-focused measurements and better competitive differentiation.

HubSpot Culture Code summarizes this concept beautifully proclaiming, "For every decision we should ask ourselves: 'Selves, what's in it for the customer?'" Profit questions have a narrow internal focus; Noble Purpose questions open the door to a bigger, more customer-driven conversation. The Noble Purpose 6-P model will help you solidify your strategy. It will help you make decisions about products, promotion, people, and process. It will help you identify the more nuanced qualitative measurements that will differentiate your organization.

Give Your Customers a Seat at the Table

If you're still on the fence about whether shifting to this type of strategy and changing your measurement systems will really make a big difference, or you're wondering how to get your boss on board, try this quick exercise.

Think about a key product or service that your organization buys on a regular basis. Maybe it's IT services, or accounting, or perhaps it's a critical product. Imagine that the contract is up for bid and you're choosing between two firms, Company A and Company B. To help you choose, you ask to sit in on one of their leadership meetings.

The leaders of Company A use a traditional 5-P model. They focus on the first set of questions; their primary lens is profit. For the leaders at Company A, you and your company are a revenue source. When you're sitting in the back of the room in their meeting, you hear them asking questions like *How can we make more money off existing customers? How can we get them to pay faster? To buy more add-ons? How can we reduce the amount of labor we spend servicing their business?*

When you visit Company B, you hear something different. Company B's leaders ask questions from the purpose list, like *How can we deliver our customers more value? How can we make it easier to do business with us? How can we train our people to be more helpful with customers?*

For them, improving your business is everything. It's what they live and breathe by.

Which supplier do you want to do business with? The answer is obvious.

What would happen if your team pretended that your best customers were in the room during their meetings? Would that change their behavior? Many firms adopt just such a practice. A 2012 *Forbes* article describes how Amazon brings the customer into the room:

> Jeff Bezos' managers at Amazon find him formidable enough. But the figure that overwhelms their lives goes by the internal nickname "the empty chair." Bezos periodically leaves one seat open at a conference table and informs all attendees that they

should consider that seat occupied by their customer, "the most important person in the room."[1]

Several of our clients use their own version of the empty chair practice as well. For example, the team at Flight Centre in Australia, whom you met earlier in the book, pride themselves on being a little crazy. Instead of leaving the chair empty, they put a life-size plastic blow-up doll in a chair to remind their team to think about the customer. Some offices have even named her, scrawling a fictional name in black marker across her forehead. There's a rumor floating around that a few have named her Lisa. (Should I be flattered or embarrassed?) Either way, it's certainly effective. Imagine being in a meeting and having your boss point to a naked blow-up doll, saying "We need to ask what she thinks about this." It makes an impression. Flight Centre's NSP—*We care about delivering amazing travel experiences*—becomes operationalized because they're intentional about giving their customers a seat at the table.

In an era of me-to-mediocrity, organizations with a laser focus on improving their customers' lives stand out. Putting your NSP at the center of your decision-making model ensures that you're asking beautiful questions, instead of exhausting question. It keeps your team focused on what matters most.

---

[1]George Anders, "Inside Amazon's Idea Machine: How Bezos Decodes Customers," *Forbes,* April 23, 2012.

9

Be For, Rather Than Against

There is nothing noble in being superior to your fellow man. True nobility lies in being superior to your former self.

—Ernest Hemingway

During a recent product launch meeting at a high-profile SaaS company, the senior leadership team rallied their troops to "kill the competition."

"We're going to obliterate them."

"We're going to make those guys worry about their mortgages!"

The team was pumped. Mouths frothed. Fists were raised. They were poised to attack. There was only one problem; at no point during the entire diatribe did anyone from the senior team ever mention the customers.

This is a serious error.

"Kill the Competition" Is Not a Rallying Cry

Focusing on beating the competition, rather than winning customers, is a common strategic error that often goes unnoticed in the heat of battle. Yet over time, this oft-made mistake stymies growth, stifles innovation, and ultimately, erodes competitive differentiation, the very thing leaders are trying to create.

We've talked about how focusing on profit stifles differentiation. Trying to kill the competition has a similar impact.

Your company has to stand for something; it can't just be against someone else. When leaders focus on killing the competition, instead of adding value to customers, the following two things inevitably happen.

Short-Term Thinking

Picture two salespeople calling on the same customer. One spends the majority of her customer face time poking holes in the competition. She drops subtle and not so subtle language about how her company is better. Because she's been well prepped by her marketing team, her comparisons are accurate.

When it comes time to present her solution, she focuses on why her products are better than the competition. She wants to beat the other guy. She wants to win the deal.

Her competitor spends his time asking the customer questions about their business. He focuses on *their* objectives. When it comes time for him to present his solution, he's able to talk about the impact his plan will have on the customer's business. He's focused on improving the customer's business *after* he wins the deal. He links his solution to the key issues most important to the customer. For him, the win is improving the customer's condition.

Who do you think will make a better business case for the customer to buy? The salesperson who focused on the competition, or the salesperson who was focused on the customer? Now the long-term questions: Who's going to have better customer intelligence to take back to their service team? Who's going to have better information to help their company sustain the business?

Who is going to have a more in-depth understanding of customer needs, which they can feed to the product development team for future innovation?

Even if the first salesperson, the kill-the-competition representative, wins the deal, she hasn't collected any customer intelligence to help her company service the account. Her service team will have to incur extra costs finding out what matters to the customer. Or more likely, they'll incur extra and unexpected costs reacting to the customer's requests, and the business will be up for bid again the following year.

When you pump up your team by bashing the competition, that's exactly what your team will discuss in front of customers. Creating a sales strategy against the competition (versus for the customers) is boring at best. Customers see it for what it is, a reactive tactic. It's intellectually lazy. It doesn't create true value for customers, or your own organization.

HubSpot, the inbound marketing term famous for their intentional and incredibly effective culture, proclaims on their Culture Code SlideShare deck, "Competitor obsession is a distraction."

Erosion of Long-Term Value

An organization focused on beating the competition is more likely to cut margin to win the business. They're not equipped to have the kind of strategic conversations with their customers that might reveal additional value opportunities because their leadership hasn't talked about customers; they've only talked about the competition. Teams focused on killing the competition rarely innovate because they don't have enough insight into their customers to come up with anything unique.

Think about people you do business with. What goes through your mind when they spend undue time discussing the failings of their competitors? Annihilating the competition is not a purpose. Customers and employees see it for what it is, a short-term grab for glory.

Decide Who You're for and Why

Jenn Adams, the Vice President of Sales for PharMEDium, says, "We've purposely chosen to focus on different things than most of our competitors."

PharMEDium is the national leader in customized pharmacy sterile compounding. A privately held firm based in Chicago, they provide products to over 3,000 acute care and primary care hospitals for patients who are the recipients of critical intravenous and epidural preparations.

Adams says, "We're in a changing regulatory environment. Some federal laws have just changed. The industry at large is mired in that. They're worried about how they're going to comply with the new laws, and how their company is going to fare. It would be very easy for us to let our internal conversations descend into checking the boxes on compliance."

Instead, Adams and her team have been intentional about shifting their end game. Adams says, "We're focused on those things (compliance), but not just on behalf of our own interest, it's for our customers. Everything we're doing around compliance is in the name of the patient. This business that we are in is serious business. There are patients at the other end of this. We always think, if this were your family member, you'd want to know that we are completely focused on getting it right 100% of the time on behalf of the patients that our customers serve every day."

PharMEDium's NSP is: "We advance patient safety and provide peace of mind." When I worked with their team developing the NSP and the associated strategy, their passion for the patients and health care providers was apparent. PharMEDium CEO Bill Spalding says, "Purpose is a vehicle to drive decision-making. When people know that patient safety is our highest value, they will not compromise for the sake of efficiency."

Adams and her team consistently win business when they're the higher priced option, because they've proven to the market that they're serious about quality and safety. Adams says, "No one is going to give you a parade for meeting your compliance goals. Our customers see that we're not just checking the box. Our customers see that we understand the importance of what we do. We are asking them to trust us, to prepare these medications on their behalf."

PharMEDium has solidified patient safety as their point of competitive differentiation. The narrative wouldn't be effective if it weren't true. PharMEDium's track record for safety is stellar. But even with a great track record, if Adams and her team hadn't been intentional about demonstrating the impact patient safety has on customers, it could have just been a number on a slide deck, another look at me feature in the marketing materials.

Many organizations tout their great numbers. Adams and her team took it further. They consistently engage in a patient-focused dialogue inside their organization. When they talk about numbers, they make a point to translate the numbers into patient impact. For example, at their 2015 banquet, when Adams presented the award to their top salesperson, she said, "This person assisted his customers in safely administering over 1,847,000 life-saving compounded sterile preparations to their patients in 2014! This winner works relentlessly to earn the trust of his customers to use PharMEDium for the benefit of their patients. Please join us in recognizing Steve, who helped over 1.8 million patients."

Imagine how proud Steve felt—he helped 1,847,000 patients!

In most organizations, the senior leader would have spotlighted Steve's sales numbers. Imagine how that would have played out. The winner would get a fabulous trip; he'd excitedly call his spouse and kids. He'd be happy. He'd buy a round of drinks for his colleagues in the bar. While his peers are congratulating him, they're probably also making a silent vow to beat him next year. *Steve had bigger sales numbers, curses, next year I'll come out on top.* The wheels of time spin, and the whole year starts again. Has anyone learned anything that will help them differentiate themselves or do a better job for customers? Probably not.

In PharMEDium's situation, everyone wins, including the customers. The winner gets to call his wife and kids and tell them that he helped 1.8 million patients. Wow. The entire rest of the team gets the message: whoever helps the most patients wins. Instead of being jealous, they're more likely to be proud of their colleague. Sure, they want to be the winner next year, but their drive isn't just to beat Steve. It's to help more patients. That's the story they take back to their territories when the meeting is over. Helping patients is what we care about and what we reward.

Mike Lapp, one of PharMEDium's top account managers says, "Our competitors aren't even thinking on our level. We're having a holistic value discussion based on a work flow analysis, and don't focus on the details of our service. Our competitors' approach is to say, 'What are you doing for morphine refills? I can save you 10 cents a unit.'

Lapp was nominated by his client Novation as National Account Manager of the year. When you get to the point where your customers are nominating you for awards, you are truly differentiated.

Adams says, "We are *not* the low-cost provider. We win business because our customers absolutely believe that we are committed to quality on their behalf, in a way that it does provide them peace of mind."

Once again, the internal conversation becomes the external conversation. It's no surprise that PharMEDium has achieved double-digit sales growth for several years in a row. Because of their success, PharMEDium was recently acquired by Amerisource-Bergen, one of the largest global pharmaceutical sourcing and distribution services company. The acquisition gives PharMEDium the leverage to scale, and improve lives for even more patients.

Adams and team changed the internal conversation, which in turn changed their perception in the market. PharMEDium doesn't direct their team to kill the competition. Instead, they say, *Save lives for our customers*. And they back it up with facts. That is how they created a tribe of True Believers.

10

Don't Confuse Culture with Collateral

The people know your motives whether you know them or not.
—Cheryl Bachelder, CEO, Popeyes

Every organization has an ethos, if not by design, then by default. The ethos is organizational spirit. It's the collective beliefs about the organization's identity and what they value. It's that intangible thing that's hard to name, yet everyone knows what it is.

It's why employees at Whole Foods know that their larger purpose is to improve health and well-being. It's why the atmosphere in some schools feels like a prison, while others hum with a creative buzz. If you walk into the principal's office, you'll likely find someone whose personal ethos has permeated the organization's culture.

As a leader, you are in absolute control of your own ethos.

Another popular definition for ethos is: The disposition, character, or fundamental values peculiar to a specific person, people, culture, or movement. You alone control your disposition, character, and values. As a leader, your personal ethos is the cornerstone of your organization's culture.

For the purpose of this book, we'll use the word *ethos* to describe beliefs, values, and aspirations, and we'll use *culture* to describe the resulting behaviors and practices of the organization.

Culture is a hot topic these days. The truism of Peter Drucker's statement, "Culture eats strategy for breakfast," is readily apparent in a knowledge economy, where your competitor can copy everything except the attitudes and actions of your people.

As a leader, your culture is more important than the goals you set because your culture determines what actually gets done. For example, if an organization sets a goal to increase on-time deliveries, but the culture tolerates excuses, it's unlikely that the team will achieve the goal. The company can provide incentives, and it may drive a short-term spike, but in the end, the culture will ultimately prevail.

When leaders try to improve their culture, they're often not sure where to start. Do you follow the cool kids in Silicon Valley, and put a foosball table in your lobby? Do you try to act like big pharma and host huge meetings where you give away trips?

We've talked about several high-performing cultures: the millennials on fire for social media at Hootsuite, the scientists passionate about patients at Roche, and the globe-trotting life changers at G Adventures. When people are asked to describe organizations with highly engaged cultures, they tend to cite well-known firms like Google or Apple. They talk about how cool their offices are with nap pods and whiteboards everywhere to capture creative thoughts. We've worked with those companies, and they are really cool. But a high-performing, everybody all-in culture is not dependent on state-of-the-art offices or sexy products. As a leader, you can create an amazing culture using nothing more than your own values and beliefs.

The true test of your culture is not your products, your website, or your office. **The true test of your culture is the employee experience.**

Earlier in the book you met Greg Thrasher, the founder of Foundation Supportworks, who started as a 20-year-old kid with a sledgehammer and pickup truck, and with the help of his wife and children, grew his business into a $100 million company.

The Thrashers don't work in software, health care, or travel. They run one of the least sexy businesses you can imagine, they work in crumbling basements. They don't have a cool office with ergonomic furniture on the bay in San Francisco. They work out of a metal building in Omaha, Nebraska. Their people aren't hipsters or highly educated scientists. Many of their people are construction workers who don't have college degrees.

Yet the Thrashers have created a culture of people who are on fire for customers. Their hourly workers volunteer their time to fix basements for needy families on the weekends. Other construction firms may hire anyone who can fog a mirror. The Thrashers put people through a rigorous interview process that includes identifying whether or not the candidate will fit their culture. Their team is filled with some of the hardest working, most engaged people I've ever met.

The Thrashers have taken their personal ethos of hard work, honesty, customer service, and kindness and scaled it into an organizational culture. Greg Thrasher says, "Finding people who share your values is the easy part. The harder part is we have taught them how to live it." They've grown their business exponentially, by being intentional about their culture.

Their success is rooted in a few key principles.

They're Avid Students of Leadership

Greg Thrasher didn't have a college education. He says, "I knew nothing about business but I knew I wanted to be an entrepreneur." He learned how to be a leader from books.

Thrasher has a monthly book club on leadership. Their offices are filled with their favorite leadership books. They don't just read them. They implement the techniques.

The Thrashers took the same learner approach to bringing their adult children into the business. Nancy says, "We learned from people who had business and who had kids that were older than ours, and were open to talking about their experiences." The Thrashers figured out what worked and what didn't. They required their children to go away to college, and work elsewhere first. Nancy says, "Our business wasn't that huge when the kids went away to college. I wanted them to see there is a bigger world than Omaha. We also told them they had to work for someone else for two to five years before they could come back."

When their sons came into the business, they didn't start at the top. They had to prove themselves in multiple positions. Because they were young, they were dealing with dealers who were decades older. Nancy says, "They had to gain credibility with the older generation, so they were motivated to read a lot." Dave Thrasher says, "For me, right out of college, working entry level, I didn't learn how to think strategically or be a leader. Even college gave me less than 2 percent of what's needed to be a successful leader. The rest came from books."

Dave says working for other companies gave him and his brother Dan perspective. He says, "You realize how tough it can be. A lot of companies can be crappy to work for, and have bad cultures. We don't take it as much for granted. Dan and I are passionate about trying to gain as much knowledge as we can. That insecurity of getting passed by keeps you reading and challenging yourself. When leaders are that passionate about learning, the employees get the message. We read, we learn, we challenge ourselves to get better."

Dave says, "I have customers who say, 'I don't like to read' or 'I'm not a good reader.' But I'm driven to be somebody special. The people at the top of their game fill themselves with the right inputs. They don't read business books for fun. They do it because they're committed to being top notch."

The Thrashers have created a culture where people know they don't have all the answers. The message is this: find expertise, read, get better. Greg says, "We've created an atmosphere where we attract people who want to continue to challenge their thinking."

They Operationalize Their Values

From the moment he got his first business cards, Greg has always put the customer first. That ethos carried over to his sons. Wife Nancy recalls, "Our kids heard Greg on the phone talking to customers. They have the enthusiasm that Greg had."

But as their business scaled, the Thrashers recognized attitude wasn't enough. Greg says, "You might plan to call a customer back, but you got so caught up you forgot about it." They put systems and processes in place to ensure that their people consistently provide top tier service. Greg says, "If your people aren't getting back to customers, it's because your system is not right. We create a system that doesn't allow you to forget."

They also work hard to build trust. Greg says, "You know in your heart you want your people to love where they work. But if you don't create an environment where you build trust, they won't." He says he's worked hard over the years to learn how to delegate more and get out of people's way.

Thrasher now has 265 employees. Their tenured employees have been with them for 10 or 15 years, but over half have been hired in the last two to three when their growth accelerated. Greg says, "We started changing a few years back. As we started thinking more about our culture, some of the older employees weren't buying into it. They just naturally moved on, or we helped them move on. Our culture is healthier now than it was five years ago."

They Give Very Personal Recognition

The Thrashers don't wait until year-end or performance review time to provide praise. They're quick to provide meaningful personal recognition when a person or team goes the extra mile. For example, Nancy says, "Our creative department has a large burden leading up to our convention." The team produced videos, graphics, and signage for the Supportworks convention that draws hundreds of dealers and their staffs from all over North America. A week before the convention, when it was crunch time, the Thrashers pulled the creative team aside. They told them how much they appreciated their work. They reminded them of how successful the past convention was. Nancy says, "I told them, we know you're working really hard, we know this is a big drag on your personal lives over the last 60 days. When this is over, the week after we get back, we'd like to take you and your spouse or guest to the nicest steakhouse in town. We want to recognize you for your hard work."

What do you think it means to a video editor who's pulling double shifts leading up to a big event to know that his boss is not only noticing his work, but planning to reward him, even before she sees the finished product? How hard do you think the team worked during that last week? To be clear, the Thrashers aren't trying to manipulate their team. Their appreciation is genuine. They want their people to know that in the moment, they see how hard they're working.

When I spoke with the Thrashers, they were in the process of planning the recognition dinner. What the employees didn't know was that in addition to the dinner, Dave Thrasher and VP of Strategy Amanda Harrington spent several hours in advance of the dinner writing up a description of how each person had contributed. Nancy says, "They don't know we're planning to talk about a person by person contribution. We are going to divide the list and say something nice about each one of them."

Dave says, "Most of the people in this department make under $50,000 a year. For them and their spouse to go out for a fancy meal, it's a place they normally wouldn't go. What's more important are the specific comments about their contributions." A small department gets personal time with the senior leaders. Each person hears the owners say something wonderful about him or her, and each spouse or guest hears it as well.

Nancy says, "If your spouse is happy with your work, if they are bought into the purpose of the company, it has a big impact."

They Overcommunicate

Dave says, "Even the best leaders have a tendency to hoard information, unintentionally." He describes how a simple parking issue can affect morale. He says, "They might not have known we were racking our brains to find more parking; all they know is they can't find a space."

He continues, "Even things we think are minute details we need to communicate to them. We need to let them know this is our vision, this is where we are headed, this is the good, this is the bad, this is the ugly. People need to know why you make the decisions you do. When they hear that, even if you don't have a good solution, they're okay with it."

When people don't know what's happening behind the scenes, it's easy to assume the leader doesn't care. Greg says, "It's almost human nature to assume bad intent. We try to overcommunicate so we don't lose their trust."

Nancy says, "We encourage spouses to get signed up for the Friday email, so they get the information." They also include births and every new employee gets his or her face in the newsletter.

They're Totally Transparent

"It's important for me to be open and share," says Greg. "Too many leaders are afraid to share who they are. If you open up as a leader yourself, it's easier for the people."

The Thrashers have created such a strong culture that their dealers, people who buy products from them, look to them for leadership training.

Greg says, "The difference between successful and unsuccessful dealers has nothing to do with geography and the market size. We have a dealer in Fargo, North Dakota doing 10 times more business than someone in a bigger city. "The ability of the owner to lead is far and away the common denominator that determines his or her success."

The Thrashers weren't always as forward thinking as they are now. "When you're at half a million or a million, you're afraid to go to the next step," says Greg. "You try to be the cheapest so you can get the job. When you're just starting out, you're afraid to sell the value. It holds you back.

"Small guys think they can't afford to hire someone talented so they hire the wrong people, and they wind up putting out fires. You have to take a risk to hire the right people."

Their focus has paid off. Their team is consistently high-ranked by consumers. Greg says, "From a long-term strategic aspect, our culture is our number one asset." The company he started with a pickup and sledgehammer is now the market leader.

Let's do a quick pause to recap. Foundation Supportworks doesn't have a cool brand or products. They're not in a sexy industry. Their people are a diverse group of blue-collar and white-collar workers across a variety of age ranges.

They have created a cohesive, high-performance, purpose-driven culture by having the discipline and persistence to apply what they learned in leadership books.

They scaled their culture across generations and traditional blue collar/white collar class lines because they were intentional about leadership. They are living proof that leadership is the key to everything.

Culture across Ages and Stages

You can't talk about culture without addressing the millennials. The generation born between 1982 and 2002 is now the largest single generation in the work force. Companies that once had no trouble keeping top talent are scratching their heads trying to figure out what kind of culture it will take to attract and retain millennials. The millennials are 34 percent of today's working population. By 2020, they'll be 46 percent of the workforce. For leaders, the millennials are a business imperative that cannot be ignored.

Millennials often get a bad rep in the corporate world. Six months here, eight months there, constantly daydreaming about what's next. Their reputation is not misplaced. A recent survey revealed that 58 percent of millennials expect to leave their jobs in three years or less; 53 percent of hiring managers say it's difficult to find and retain millennials.

Yet while many leaders are frustrated with millennials, other leaders find their perspective refreshing.

When the following article, written by my millennial daughter Elizabeth McLeod, originally ran on Forbes.com and LinkedIn Pulse, it went viral. As of this writing, the article has 1.3 million views, becoming one of LinkedIn's top 20 articles **ever.** It hit a hot button. Thousands of comments poured in. They ranged from the disgusted to the effusive. Leaders responded in one of two ways. Some said, "Purpose is what everyone wants." While other said, "These kids want everything now, don't they understand paying your dues?" The millennials said, "I want my work to mean something today, not 10 years from now."

Their responses illustrated the differences and commonalities in generations. Both groups yearn for a higher purpose; the younger group wants to experience it now. Their elders believe it comes with accomplishment.

On this one, I'm inclined to side with the millenials. Why should you have to wait to feel like your work matters? Steve Johnson of Hootsuite says, "The thing I really appreciate about these younger workers is they look at it and say, 'Life's too short. If it's not aligned around my purpose I'm going to go somewhere else.'"

Why Millennials Keep Dumping You: An Open Letter to Management

You hired us thinking this one might be different; this one might be in it for the long haul. We're six months in, giving everything we have; then suddenly, we drop a bomb on you. We're quitting.

Attracting and keeping top millennial talent is a hot topic because it's difficult, and so few leaders have mastered it. We know the stereotypes. Millennials never settle down. We are drowning in debt for useless degrees. We never put our phone away. We are addicted to lattes even at the expense of our water bill. Baby boomers aren't wrong about these perceptions. But pointing to our sometimes irresponsible spending and fear of interpersonal commitment isn't going to solve your problem. You still need us. We're 35 percent of the workforce; by 2020 we'll be 46 percent of the workforce. We're the ones who have mastered social media, who have the energy of a thousand suns, who will knock back five-dollar macchiatos until the job is done perfectly.

I've worked in corporate America, administrative offices, advertising agencies, and restaurants. I've had bosses ranging from 24 to 64. I've had bosses I loved, and bosses I didn't. I've seen my peers quit and have quit a few times myself. I've seen my fair share of baby boomers wondering, "What happened?" Now, I'm going to tell you what's really behind your millennials' resignation letter:

1. **You tolerate low-performance.**

    It's downright debilitating to a high achiever. I'm working my heart out and every time I look up Donna-Do-Nothing is contemplating how long is too long to take for lunch. I start wondering why leadership tolerates this.

    Is that the bar here? No thanks.

2. **ROI is not enough for me.**

I spent Sunday thinking about how I can make a difference to our clients. Now it's Monday morning, what do I hear? Stock price. Billing. ROI. Suddenly, my Monday power playlist seems useless. I'm sitting in a conference room listening to you drag on about cash flow.

I was making more money bartending in college than I am at this entry-level job. So I'll get a raise in a year if the company hits a certain number? So what? I need something to care about TODAY. Talk to me about how we make a difference, not your ROI report.

3. **Culture is more than free Panera.**

Yes. I am a cash-strapped millennial who REALLY appreciates free lunches, T-shirts, and even pens. But too often, corporate leaders confuse culture with collateral. I don't wake up at 6 a.m. every day to play foosball in the break room. I'm not inspired to be more innovative over a Bacon Turkey Bravo.

I need to be surrounded by people who are on fire for what we are doing. I need a manager who is motivated to push boundaries and think differently. Working in a cool office is really awesome. So is free lunch. But a purposeful culture is more important.

4. **It's okay to get personal.**

Treat me like a number? I'll return the favor. This job will quickly become nothing more than my rent payment. I'll start living for Friday and counting down the minutes until 5. After a few months of that, I'll probably have a drunken epiphany and realize I want more out of my life than this.

Then I'll prove your assumptions right. Eight months in, I'll quit and leave. Or worse, I'll quit and stay, just like Donna-Do-Nothing.

(continued)

(continued)

That's not good for either of us. Here's what you need to know:

I was raised to believe I can change the world. I'm desperate for you to show me that the work we do here matters, even just a little bit. I'll make copies, I'll fetch coffee, I'll do the grunt work. But I'm not doing to help you get a new Mercedes.

I'll give you everything I've got, but I need to know it makes a difference to something bigger than your bottom line.

Signed,

Your Future Best Employee

Companies like Hootsuite attract and retain top millennial talent because they've intentionally built their cultures around purpose rather than hierarchy. For the record, Hootsuite is a young company, but as they've grown they attracted plenty of baby boomers and others who want to be part of something exciting.

As you saw in the key trends outlined earlier in the book, the emotional expectations of the self-help movement are now firmly entrenched in the workplace. People are no longer willing to give up meaning today, for a potential promotion 20 years down the line.

A purpose-driven culture has cross-generational appeal. Millennials want to make a difference now because they were raised to believe they could change the world. Workers in the heavy stages of family obligations want to know their work is more than just a paycheck. When you're juggling multiple demands, meaningful work gives you the energy to cope. Boomers are thinking about their legacies. What value did they add through their life's work?

As a leader, when you're intentional about your culture, you create a team of people who know how to make good decisions when you're not there. Leaving your culture to chance can be deadly.

The GM Salute

In 2014, a GM ignition switch defect resulted in the deaths of 13 people. When the National Highway Traffic Safety Administration released the 315-page report investigating how the GM product defects occurred, it exposed a leader's worst nightmare, a culture of inertia and incompetence. The defects and poor decisions that went unreported to senior leaders ultimately caused the deaths of 13 General Motors customers. GM CEO Mary Barra, who had been in her job for less than six months when the report was issued, inherited an organization where lower-ranking employees made poor decisions or did nothing about critical safety issues. In a June 5, 2014 Town Hall, Barra said, "Repeatedly, individuals failed to disclose critical pieces of information that could have fundamentally changed the lives of those impacted by a faulty ignition switch."[1]

Barra took responsibility for fixing the GM culture moving forward. An electrical engineer by training who has worked for General Motors since she was an 18-year co-op student, Barra is an ambitious go-getter who successfully led, at different points in her career, Human Resources and Product Development. I'm sure she was flabbergasted that GM employees would be so apathetic.

Such is the challenge of leadership. You often inherit people who have completely different values from yours. Barra rose to the top because of her talent, work ethic, and values. But that doesn't mean all of her colleagues emulated the same traits. The culture that precedes you will dominate daily behavior and decision-making, unless you make proactive efforts to change it.

In the Valukas Report, the 315-page document summarizing the investigation into the company's handling of a defective ignition, one of the most colorful descriptions of the cultural morass

---

[1]"GM CEO Mary Barra's Remarks to Employees on Valukas Report Findings," Gm Corporate Newsroom, June 5, 2014.

came from Barra herself. She described for investigators a phenomenon known as the "GM nod." The GM nod, Barra described, is "when everyone nods in agreement to a proposed plan of action, but then leaves the room with no intention of follow through," the report reads. "It is an idiomatic recognition of a culture that does not move issues forward quickly, as the story of the Cobalt demonstrates."

There was also the "GM salute," described by another interviewee as "a crossing of the arms and pointing outward toward others, indicating that the responsibility belongs to someone else, not me."

The Valukas Report made it clear that the culture at GM was anything but intentional. Barra didn't create it, but she certainly inherited it. Employees continually received mixed message about the most critical issues. The report reads, "Repeated throughout the interview process we heard from GM personnel two somewhat different directives, 'When safety is an issue, cost is irrelevant' and 'cost is everything.'" If you were a GM employee, which one of these two messages would you heed? Cost is irrelevant where safety is concerned? Or cost is everything?

GM's mission statement (taken from their website at the time of the incidents) provides some clues as to which message was most important:

> GM is a multinational corporation engaged in socially responsible operations, worldwide. It is dedicated to providing products and services of such quality that our customers will receive superior value, while our employees and business partners will share in our success and our stockholders will receive sustained superior returns on their investments.

It's benign enough. Like many mission statements it talks about products, value, stakeholders, and shareholders. That's the problem. It tries to address everything, and by doing so it actually addresses nothing.

Is there anything in that mission statement that tells you the single driving force of the company? It's not without accident that the last phrase is, "stockholders will receive sustained superior returns on their investments." One thing every writer knows: the last phrase is the most important. It's what you want people to remember.

If you tell employees that safety is your top priority, yet they know that hitting the earnings target is what really matters, they're going to behave accordingly. Employees know what they need to pay attention to and what to ignore.

It's kind of like when you were a kid, and your mom said, "We're going to clean up this house from top to bottom," you knew whether you were in for a week of scrubbing toilets with a toothbrush or if the effort would be abandoned by lunch. In the case of my mom, proclamations made during the family meetings were serious business, but any instructions given after 5 p.m., when she had a glass of wine in her hand, could safely be ignored.

We didn't write down the rules in a kid codebook; we just knew from years of intuitively figuring out "how things work" in our house. We knew it didn't matter what my mother said; after 5 p.m. her real goal was relaxation.

In business, unspoken beliefs about the leader's "real goals" can create a culture where it is entirely possible for the leader to direct people to do one thing, and have the team respond by doing the exact opposite.

I don't think there's a single person at GM who wanted this to happen. But in the absence of a clear purpose, the culture will drive behavior because employees are left guessing what management really wants.

What if GM had an NSP like this:

We make vehicles that thrill people and keep them safe.

Would this statement let employees know exactly what matters most? If senior leadership told you, "This is our North Star, we want to thrill consumers and keep them safe," how would you respond if you saw someone compromising safety? What about product development? If your purpose was to thrill consumers, would you be okay with average products? What about features that didn't work well, or unmet customer needs—would you be okay with the status quo? What if you were in purchasing, would you buy the same old stuff, or would you push your suppliers to make it better, more exciting, and safer?

A clear purpose won't create a culture for you, but it's a good start. While the stakes were higher for GM than most, we shouldn't continue to be surprised by these situations. A culture focused entirely on quarterly earnings will never be anything other than an every-man-for-himself rat race.

Consider the case of Volkswagen. In September 2015, the U.S. Environmental Protection Agency found that Volkswagen deliberately programmed some 500,000 diesel-powered vehicles to provide false readings during emissions testing. Volkswagen engineers created a "defeat device," software in diesel engines that could detect when they were being tested. Dubbed "diesel dupe," the scandal resulted in the immediate resignation of Volkswagen CEO Martin Winterkorn.

Prior to the fraud, it was widely known that Winterkorn's long-standing goal was to overtake Toyota and become the world's biggest automaker. After eight years with Winterkorn at the helm, Volkswagen's revenues surpassed Toyota in early 2015. It's not without coincidence that Winterkorn framed Volkswagen's goal as an internally-driven financial objective (bigger, beat Toyota) versus a customer-impact metric like quality or satisfaction.

The team at Volkswagen knew their purpose was to beat Toyota, not in quality, but in revenue. Are we surprised that Winterkorn's team decided the best use of their engineering talent was to find a way to lie about problems, rather than solve them? It's the logical consequence of an organization whose sole purpose is increasing revenue.

It has yet to be determined whether Winterkorn knew about the issue. However, as CEO for eight years, he is responsible for a culture where people believed that beating Toyota was more important than complying with the law.

Volkswagen is paying a heavy price for their ethics failure. Industry experts say fines, private settlements, recall costs, and future loss of sales will cost Volkswagen a minimum of $34.5 billion. They've gone from being a trusted source of engineering excellence to being the least trusted brand, overnight. Time will tell what the future holds for the team at Volkswagen.

They could take a lesson from Mary Barra. She was absolutely honest during the investigation. At an economic club event one year later, she described how she is shifting the organization's focus to customers. "By listening carefully to their hopes, their concerns, and their expectations, and then applying the talent and resources that we have, we can demonstrate that customers are truly at the center of everything we do."

Barra has since fired 15 employees for failing to take responsibility, and is reframing GM's culture around a higher purpose than just money. On their investor website, GM now says, "Our purpose begins with a few simple but very powerful words, *we are here to earn customers for life.*" Operationalizing this aspiration will be a challenge for Barra. Publicly announcing that GM has a higher purpose beyond money is a great start.

We live in an age of transparency. People are going to know your values, whether you announce them or not. As a Noble Purpose leader you have to declare your purpose and intentionally build your culture around it. The true mark of a leader is how your team makes decisions when you're not there. Creating a Noble Purpose culture ensures that your team will do the right thing, even when no one's watching.

11

Take "Yes, But" Off the Table

Once you replace negative thoughts with positive ones, you'll start having positive results.

—Willie Nelson

In some industries, it's harder to create positive cultures than in others. Phil Moore, the managing partner of Porter Keadle Moore, an Atlanta-based accounting firm, says, "As accountants, our job is to find the bad stuff that other people can't see, so it's easy for our default to be negative."

When Porter Keadle Moore was founded in 1997, they worked primarily with life insurance companies. They expanded into community banking, and now PKM (as they're known) currently represents corporations in the financial, insurance, technology and biological science, commercial, and government service arenas. Their NSP is *We help clients seize opportunities and reduce risk.*

Their clients are in high-risk situations. PKM's role is to help them be successful, while at the same time, to avoid problems. Moore says, "You get a bunch of accountants, or engineers, or lawyers together, and it's not going to be as positive as a roomful of PR or marketing people." He describes the DNA of accountants saying, "We put ourselves in a position where our default wiring is finding problems, or at least we've tended to believe that's our job. Our culture, the nature of our business, is about finding the problems with performance. We have trained ourselves to look for the bad stuff."

Moore, along with senior partner and COO Debbie Sessions, recognized that their firm was not unique. Most accounting firms have a problem-oriented culture. Yet Moore and Sessions knew that firm growth was dependent upon the partners' abilities to sell the firm in a positive way. Most accounting firms talk about their history and their skills, but those are merely table stakes. Moore and Sessions were looking for a way to differentiate their firm. And it had to start with the 13 partners.

Moore and Sessions needed to elevate the cultural wiring of the firm. They wanted to rally their team around their ability to improve their client's business. Moore and Sessions recognized that their firm wasn't good at celebrating success. Whenever someone brought in a new client, the partners immediately dissected the deal looking for all the potential problems. Lack of celebration has a chilling effect on the ability to develop new business. Without a positive framing on the deals they'd closed, the partners didn't have a differentiated narrative to carry out into the balance of the firm or into the field when they were looking for new business.

Moore and Sessions decided to institute the "Yes AND rule." Moore says, "In the past, someone would share a success, and the response was Yes, but, then a laundry list of the things that could go wrong." Moore and Sessions reframed their weekly partners meeting, no more *Yes, but*, only *Yes AND*. For the first 15 minutes of the weekly meeting the team shared successes. Not a negative word could be spoken. When they landed a new audit client, the partner described the deal, and the others chimed in:

Yes AND it's exactly the kind of client we want.

Yes AND the work will be profitable.

Yes AND we can put some of our new people on the project.

Moore says, "It changed the air in the room. We took the comma off the table, no more Yes, but, only Yes AND."

That simple exercise of Yes AND shifted the team's brain patterns. Much like when G Adventures ignited the frontal lobes of their travel agents, Moore and Sessions were tapping into the brain science of motivation. Small wins have a big impact on motivation.

If you're ever found yourself playing solitaire or Angry Birds longer than you'd planned, you've experienced this sensation. In *The Progress Principle*, psychologists Teresa Amabile and Steven Kramer reveal what the designers of video and computer games have known for years. People will become strongly motivated (and even "addicted") to games that allow a sense of small accomplishments: getting to the next level, finishing a challenging quest or task, solving a problem, or overcoming a foe.

As a leader, putting a system in place to celebrate small wins enables your team to experience quick hits of the brain chemical dopamine. The *Psychology Today* website defines dopamine as "a neurotransmitter that helps control the brain's reward and pleasure centers. Dopamine also helps regulate movement and emotional responses, and it enables us not only to see rewards, but to take action to move toward them."

Rather than relying on video games or an after-work drink for a hit of dopamine, celebrating small wins fills your team with energy. It improves their resilience for future challenges. Moore says, "We get to the problems later; that's part of our job."

Moore and Sessions are intentional about how they run their partners meetings. They start with the celebration, which sets the context and tone. We're a successful firm that's winning deals. Then they move into operational issues, which tend to be more challenging. Having experienced the positive, the partners address the challenges with more confidence. Since they began the "Yes AND" technique, celebrating their quick wins, there is no less rigor to their dissection of issues. The difference is the mental confidence and optimism the partners bring to the process. Sessions says, "If anything, they dive deeper, because it doesn't seem as exhausting."

Moore and Sessions also make sure to end the weekly meetings on a high note. They look at their opportunities and summarize their biggest wins of the week. Sessions says, "We're intentional about the order, so it doesn't go rolling off the mountain top. We start on top and we finish on top."

Resetting the Negative

Moore and Sessions are smart. Rather than simply telling their team to be more positive, they created a process to ignite positive energy. One of the prevailing elements in dysfunctional cultures is negativity. You've probably seen the studies revealing that it takes five positive interactions to counteract one negative comment.

This work began with noted psychologist John Gottman's exploration of positive-to-negative ratios in marriages. Gottman dubbed the 5:1 ratio the *magic ratio*. As long as there are five times as many positive interactions between partners as there are negative interactions, the relationship is likely to be stable. Gottman and his colleagues observed 700 newlywed couples for one 15-minute interaction. Scoring their positive and negative interactions in *a single 15-minute conversation* between each husband and wife, Gottman and his colleagues predicted whether they would stay together or divorce. Ten years later, the follow-up revealed that they had predicted divorce with 94 percent accuracy.

The same principles apply to business. If your team is experiencing negativity, it will derail them. They'll either divorce you (quit), or they'll institute an emotional separation (quit and stay). As a leader, you must do more than just provide positive feedback, you have to fight against the "Yes, buts."

Let's go back to marriage. One thing I continually observe in unhappy couples is that they can't let a compliment for their spouse stand. If you say, "He's really great with the kids," they respond, "Yes, but he leaves a mess every time they do something." It's almost as though they feel the compliment is a violation of the truth. It's incomplete information. They can't let that incomplete information just sit there without pointing out the full story.

That's what was happening at Porter Keadle Moore. Prior to Sessions and Moore's Yes AND reframe, their team of accountants was unable to let the positive information stand alone. They felt compelled to fill in the rest of the story with a *Yes, but.*

As a leader, when you start to talk about purpose, you're going to hear a lot of *Yes, buts.*

Yes, purpose is great, but we still have to make money.

Yes, customers are critical, but so are our shareholders.

Yes, inspiring people is good, but we still need metrics.

Yes, we want to make a difference to customers, but we can't do it every time.

You need to turn these into Yes ANDs. The above statements are not pairs of conflicting ideas. The first idea in each sentence is not an opposing idea from the second one. Yet people will tell you, these two things cannot exist at the same time.

The human mind is a belief engine. We constantly look for evidence that reinforces our existing beliefs. Our minds also love to create dichotomies. We split issues apart because it makes them easier for us to understand. For example, many people believe you can't combine accountability with compassion, or that safety and creativity can exist in the same plane. Yet there is significant evidence that these things can be combined for extraordinary results. Excellent leaders are compassionate *and* they hold people accountable. Disney combines safety and what they refer to as show (creativity) to thrill and delight their theme park customers. People and organizations who embrace a both/and mentality fare better than those who succumb to the default brain pattern of either/or. Creating a false dichotomy between issues like profit and purpose or caring and accountability results in a less effective organization. It creates the *Yes, but* culture.

The *Yes, but* problem also stems from our need for safety. The amygdala, the most primitive part of the brain, commonly referred to as the lizard brain, is always on the lookout for danger. A holdover from our prehistoric ancestors, your lizard brain is constantly scanning the environment for the modern-day version of a saber-toothed tiger. Unfortunately, the lizard brain isn't very smart; it can't tell the difference between a threat to your life and a threat to your ego. To the lizard brain, a threat is a threat. A saber-toothed tiger and a change in policy register as the same thing. We've survived as a species by spotting danger before it strikes. Erring on the side of fear will keep you alive. But it doesn't necessarily make you a better leader. And it will never make your team more creative or engaged.

Think about this combination of conditions:

- The brain is constantly looking for evidence that our current beliefs are correct.
- The human mind creates false dichotomies to make life easier.
- Anticipating problems, even if they might not be there, keeps you safe.

As you look at this list, are you surprised that *Yes, but* is a frequent default response in business and life? As you consider the above truisms of human nature, it's easy to become disheartened. Don't be.

Yes, human beings can be frustrating, AND, it is also a truism of human nature that people are capable of change. We have hard evidence that time and time again, people can overcome their lesser instincts to produce greatness.

The famed cultural anthropologist Margaret Meade once said, "Never doubt that a small group of thoughtful, committed citizens can change the world; indeed, it's the only thing that ever has."

If you want to change the air in your organization, be the leader who takes *Yes, but* off the table. Noble Purpose brings strategy and spirit together. It is not always an easy or obvious mix. Don't let your team descend into a false dichotomy. As Cheryl Bachelder, CEO of Popeyes, whom you'll meet in the next chapter, says, "The dynamic tension between daring and serving creates the conditions for superior performance."

As the leader, you must have absolute clarity. Purpose and profit are linked. You will achieve your purpose on many days, *and* you will also fail.

Taking *Yes, but* off the table gives your team the opportunity to celebrate their wins. A leader who embraces Yes AND creates the conditions for excellence.

12

The Folly of Internal Customers

There is only one boss. The customer. And he can fire everyone from the chairman on down simply by spending his money somewhere else.
—Sam Walton

Does your team talk about internal customers? If so, it can have a chilling effect on your performance.

The concept of internal customers sounds good in theory. It goes something like this: employees who don't interact with external customers have internal customers, key stakeholders for whom they provide services. The IT department may consider the field their internal customers; finance may serve operations, and so.

But let's be honest, how many times have you seen someone break a sweat for an internal customer? People want to please internal customers, but they know in their hearts, they're not the same as paying customers.

The internal customer is an artificial construct designed to improve cooperation between departments. But it rarely sparks urgency. In fact, I would go so far as to say the very concept of internal customers waters down urgency for real customers.

It can drive organizational mediocrity because internal customers never hold the same consequences as external customers. When everyone is a "customer," the passion, commitment, and urgency for real customers, the people who pay for and use your services, diminishes.

Look at the average corporate mission statement. It's usually some version of:

> We strive to be number one in our markets by providing excellent products and services to our employees, stakeholders, community, and shareholders.

It's milquetoast messaging that says, "We want to be all things to all people and be nice while we're doing it." This type of mission statement provides absolutely no direction whatsoever.

Without a clearly defined purpose, each department is left to their own devices, with people are all over the place and no organizational alignment (Figure 12.1).

Clarity about what your purpose is and who your customers are points everyone in your organization in the same direction (Figure 12.2).

In his departure email, Andrew Mason, the former CEO of Groupon wrote, "Have the courage to start with the customer. My biggest regrets are the moments that I let a lack of data override my intuition on what's best for our customers."

In Chapter 11, we saw how the General Motors "we serve everyone" mission created a mixed message, and enabled a culture where safety standards eroded. As a Noble Purpose leader, you have to decide who your customers are, and who they are not. Everyone in your organization needs to know exactly who you're serving.

Sometimes, the not so obvious choice is the best one.

Learning to Love People You Don't Even Like

Popeyes Louisiana Kitchen Inc. is an Atlanta-based multibillion-dollar chain of 220 restaurants around the world. When Cheryl

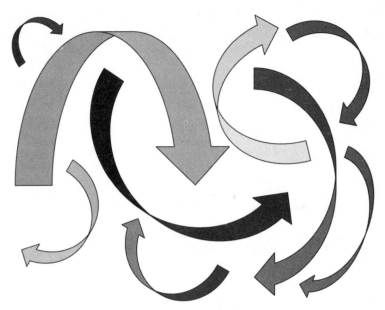

Figure 12.1   Lack of Organizational Alignment

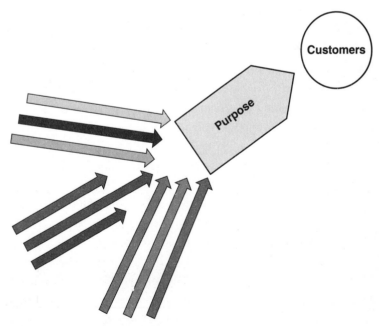

Figure 12.2   Goals Aligned Toward Customer

Bachelder became CEO in 2007, Popeyes was a struggling restaurant chain with a long history of declining sales and profits. Leadership had been a revolving door of CEOs—four in seven years. In those same seven years, guest traffic had declined. Same store sales were negative. Average unit volume and profitability had fallen to dangerously low levels. The relationship between the company and its franchisees was on the rocks. Every data point they measured was going the wrong way. The stock price had slid from a peak of $34 per share in 2002 to $13 on the day Bachelder joined the company in 2007.

If you were the leader in that situation, what would you do first?

When Bachelder took the helm at Popeyes there was intense pressure to turn around the failing organization. There were a million places to start. Many leaders in Bachelder's situation would have focused on earnings, revenue, operations, or, at the very least, product development.

But Bachelder made a bold decision. Instead of jumping into operations, she decided to conduct what she refers to as a "grand experiment in leadership."

She says, "What if we were able to prove that a daring aspiration and selfless service to others could deliver superior performance results? What if purpose and a set of principles could guide us to industry-leading performance? What if we did this under the scrutiny of a public-company environment, garnering the attention of those cynical, short-term Wall Street investors?"

Prior to joining Popeyes, Bachelder's leadership philosophy had been brewing for years. She says, "About 15 years ago I began studying leadership intensely." She was fascinated by the "Level V Leadership" principles Jim Collins documented in *Good to Great*. The paradoxical mix of personal humility and professional will that drove exceptional results established the business case for servant leadership. During her 30-year career with organizations like Procter & Gamble, Kentucky Fried Chicken, and Yum brands, Bachelder worked for a wide range of people: some great leaders and some terrible leaders. She'd looked at the traits of the leaders she loved—the ones for whom she had worked the hardest, who had brought out the best performance. She asked herself, "What kind of leader do I aspire to become?"

While her career arc is impressive, she says, "I have not always enjoyed success as a leader. In the fall of 2003, unable to sustain a turnaround of KFC restaurants, my boss suggested it was time for me to leave. In other words, I got fired. Few things are as clarifying as losing your job. My confidence was shaken. It was unsettling. It forced a lot of reflection. But I came out a better leader."

Bachelder had personal trials as well. She describes the pain of losing her father, her mentor, Daddy Max as she called him, whom she adored. "I was brought to my knees by trials," she says. She emerged thinking, "Why not be brave?"

In the spring of 2007, Bachelder was ready to be brave. With her board's support, Bachelder began her grand experiment in leadership. Bachelder was going to make the duality of daring aspirations and selfless service the cornerstone of leadership strategy at Popeyes. But first, she and her team had to decide who they were actually going to serve. In her book, *Dare to Serve*, Bachelder writes,

> If we are going to serve people well at Popeyes—whom would we serve?
>
> We listed all the possibilities on the conference room flip chart: the guests, the shareholders, the franchise owners, the team members, the board of directors, the regulators, and the accountants. Had we missed anyone?
>
> Someone said, "Don't we have to serve all of those people?"
> Hmmm. Could be true. Let's go through each possibility.

The team went through the list. For many franchise organizations, shareholders and investors are the end game. The franchisees are viewed as a source of revenue for the corporation. Other organizations focus on store guests because they're paying customers. Bachelder and her team made a very different decision; they decided that they would serve their franchise owners.

She writes, "Franchise owners do the heavy lifting. They had made sizable investments and were committed by contract to operate our brand. If they did not prosper, there was no chance Popeyes' sales would go up (royalties) or franchisee fees would increase (new openings). Either franchise owners would succeed or Popeyes would fail."

To an outsider, this might not seem like a radical decision. But in the franchise world, it's unique. The restaurant industry in particular has a long history of contentious relationship between franchisors and franchisees. Bachelder writes, "When I joined Domino's Pizza in 1995, Domino's franchisees sued the company in a class-action lawsuit. When I joined KFC in 2001, I learned of the long history of conflict between KFC franchisees and the franchisor, with a negotiation settlement in 1996. The media has reported on troubled franchisee/franchisor relationship at well-known brands such as Burger King, Quiznos, and others."

Talk to any franchisor or franchisee, in the restaurant business or otherwise, and you'll likely get an earful of grumbling about the other side. Popeyes was no different. At the time Bachelder and her team decided to serve their franchisees, the franchisees were mad and "sick and tired" of bad results. Bachelder says, "My first day on the job involved standing on a huge stage in front of the business owners [franchisees] with a teleprompter and a Power-Point presentation. Looking back I probably should have worn a bulletproof vest."

In her TEDx talk, "Dare to Serve," Bachelder describes the Popeyes mindset toward franchisees when she started:

"On that given day we didn't even like these people. Honest to goodness, have you ever met a franchisee? They're really passionate; they've got more opinions than you can count. When they're upset, they're difficult to be with. They can be really challenging.

"This was the mindset of Popeyes seven years ago. The most important people in our business model were not our favorite people. More important than the decision we made to serve them, was to actually decide to love them. To love them for making those investments in our brand. To love them for the passion they have about the future of this brand. To love them enough to listen to them and work with them side by side to make this brand successful. That decision to love differentiated us from our competitors."

Fast forward to today. Popeyes restaurants have experienced seven years of growth. Market share has grown from 14 to 21 percent. The profitability of restaurants has improved 40 percent. The stock price is now in the $40 range—up 450 percent. The company is now the darling of the industry. Bachelder was named by CNBC's Jim Kramer as one of his "21 Bankable CEOs" for 2014.

The decision to serve franchisees wasn't easy for Bachelder and her team. There was a long history of mistrust and broken promises. Bachelder writes, "I've come to understand the similarity between working with franchisee owners and parenting an adopted child (which she has also done). Because of the history of distrust in their early life, they may never trust you—but you can still lead them, love them, and serve them well."

Popeyes did a whole host of things very well, but Bachelder says one of the most important things was being specific about their end game. Her advice to other leaders is "Consciously decide who you will serve. Don't leave this to chance."

The franchisees weren't the traditional industry choice. But they were the smartest choice. Not only did they control the success or failure of Popeyes via their execution of the brand and strategy, they were also directly involved in the revenue chain.

When companies try to serve too many constituents, people become removed from the direct revenue chain. Choosing a clearly defined group who were a direct line in the revenue chain gave Popeyes a laser focus.

Their decision to love a group that many people didn't even like took their aspirations even further. As with other organizations we've looked at, the rise in stock price didn't happen immediately. The rise in earnings followed a change in culture. In 2013, six years into Bachelder's grand experiment, 95 percent of Popeyes franchisees rated the overall quality of the Popeyes system as good, very good, or excellent, a 50 percent improvement over the 2008 owner survey. That same year, 93 percent of franchise owners said they would invest in Popeyes again.

Bachelder's decision to brave and love her franchisees paid off. Many leaders shy away from using the word *love* in a leadership context. I find this ironic because even non-emotional leaders use the word love in business all the time.

We want our customer to love our products.

We want the market to love our stock.

We want employees to love their jobs.

In the above context, love is expressed as an outcome. It's something you get in exchange for your best effort. Many leaders may be more comfortable with this context, but real leadership doesn't work that way. If you want your customers and your team to love you, you have to love them first. For exceptional leaders, love isn't an outcome, it's an action.

Bachelder and her team at Popeyes didn't shy away from loving their franchisees. One reason they were able to do it so successfully is because they were intentional in choosing their constituents. They didn't try to pretend that they were going to serve everyone. They directed their entire organization towards a single group.

Other firms we've discussed have been equally intentional. Roche chose patients as their end game. G Adventures focused on travel agents. Flight Centre chose the travelers.

Look at your own organization. Do you and your team know who your real customers are? Have you made a choice about who you serve? Lack of clarity about who your customers are creates organizational malaise.

As a leader, you have to decide at the end of the day: Who are we really for? Your ultimate customer should be people who are directly involved in your revenue loop. Be as specific as you possibly can. If prior to this point you've been focusing on everyone, you're probably going to get some pushback when you try to narrow your focus. Keep in mind, focusing on one group doesn't mean that you don't care about the others. Bachelder and her team work with franchisees to enhance the guest experience. The team at Roche emotionally engages with physicians by telling patient stories. Choosing a specific constituency provides a focused lens on your business. It helps you craft a clear and compelling NSP.

Being specific about who your customers are, and who they are not, will likely require that you abandon some of your previous habits and vernacular.

Stop Talking about Internal Customers, Start Talking about Winning

Think about sports teams or the military. You never hear a soccer fullback saying, "I'm passing the ball to the forward because she's my internal customer, and I want her to be delighted by my service." Can you imagine a navy airplane mechanic saying, "The pilots are my internal customers, I strive to give them excellent service."

Hell no.

Instead they say, "I've got my buddy's back because I want to win." The real game is out there, not in here. Even leaders in non-customer-facing roles must be clear about who their organization ultimately serves.

Connect the Dots to Actual Human Beings

One of our clients, Dave Myers, is the EVP and Chief Customer Officer of Seneca Medical, a medical-surgical product supply company. A few years ago, Dave's mother went into the hospital. Sitting in her hospital room, when it was touch and go, Dave realized, at that moment, that he wasn't just a supply chain guy; he was a son who loved his mother. Yet as he looked at the equipment, tubes, and medicines saving her life, he realized, "Many of these products have passed through the hands of my team."

Now when Dave speaks to his team, he says, "Every time you touch one of the boxes, you are holding someone's mother's life in your hands." While other companies are saying we need more inventory turns to satisfy our stakeholders, Dave Myers says, "Packing and shipping these boxes, getting the blocking and tackling right, can be the difference between someone's mother living or dying."

Which warehouse workers will care more about their jobs? The team trying to hit a number to satisfy their internal customers? Or the team who knows that being 100 percent accurate can save a life?

Dave's company doesn't make products; they distribute them. But, like the leaders at Explorys and Roche, humanizing the end patients brings them to life for people who might otherwise be removed.

Correlate Nonperformance to Customer Impact

Early in my career, I worked in a sales office where one of the administrative assistants was consistently rude to everyone. (Everyone except our boss, that is.) Anyone who spoke to an actual customer that way would have been fired on the spot. But, because she was an internal person, dealing with other internal people, it was tolerated.

Yet even though she never spoke directly to customers, she had a chilling effect on those who did. We never asked her for reports or help on presentations, things that were technically her responsibility and that would have helped us provide better service to actual customers or win more deals. Instead, as her "internal customers," we merely grumbled and did the work ourselves. If we had been savvier, we would have documented exactly how her performance was negatively impacting our paying customers. I suspect our boss would have been shocked, and likely taken action.

Top-tier organizations don't tolerate mediocrity because the stakes are too high. Nonperformers are coached or dismissed because everyone knows: the real win is about creating success for customers.

As a Noble Purpose leader, your actions, your policies, and your culture must be aligned around the impact you want to have on customers. You must choose who they are and how you want to affect them.

Bachelder says, "Perhaps you think selfless service is for charitable causes and saints. Perhaps you think serving is weak and cowardly not bold and courageous. It's time to reconsider your assumptions."

In the fall of 2001, three years after they began their turnaround, Popeyes created their purpose. They chose that time because the turnaround was well under way. Bachelder says, "While we believed the work we were doing was purposeful, we weren't sure the rest of the organization shared our conviction. Maybe it was purposeful for us, but 'just a job' for them. We analyzed what we had done well and what we needed to do next. We realized we had not explained to our followers why the work we were doing was important—why we passionately believe in the future of Popeyes."

Bachelder and her team recognized that their success had been driven by their unique leadership approach. They had embraced the dynamic tension between daring and serving, and that model had created superior results. They realized that their purpose was to inspire others to do the same. They recognized: "We are in the service business—and we celebrate that fact." Understanding how they impact their customers (franchisees), how they've done it differently from other people in the industry, and what they were personally passionate about, they declared the purpose of their work at Popeyes:

Inspire servant leaders to achieve superior results.

Bachelder says, "It is the leader's responsibility to bring purpose and meaning to the work of the organization." Bachelder herself teaches a class in personal purpose for employees, to help them connect the organizational purpose to their personal purpose.

Bachelder elaborates, "In my leadership journey, I have uncovered something that, in your heart of hearts, you already know. The motives of great leaders go beyond self-interest. They shun the spotlight in favor of serving a higher purpose."

Bachelder is proof that compassion and accountability are not mutually exclusive. She says, "The numbers don't lie. The numbers hold you accountable to making real improvements."

The internal customer is a well-intended concept that drives mediocrity. Real customers are the people who pay you, and use your services; they're the people everyone in your organization should focus on.

Bachelder says, "One of the reasons no one declares a purpose is because they would have to be held accountable."

Choosing to be one thing means choosing not to be something else. It will prevent you from taking certain types of work, and it will keep you from going after every opportunity. If your choosing a constituency and solidifying your purpose doesn't eliminate options for you, then you haven't been clear enough.

13 | Name Your Noble Sales Purpose

Definiteness of purpose is the starting point of all achievement.
—W. Clement Stone

It's become popular for leaders to talk about their "Why." But you can't simply say, "We make a difference" and assume everyone will know how to do it. If you want to fully leverage the power of purpose, you have to name your purpose and then operationalize it.

Now that you understand the concept of an NSP—Noble Sales Purpose—and how you'll use it, it's time to create your own.

You'll start with the three big discovery questions:

1. How do you make a difference to your customers?
2. How do you do it differently from your competition?
3. On your best day, what do you love about your job?

When we work with senior teams, we assign these questions in advance. We tell people, "We're looking for big answers. We don't want marketing speak or a side by side comparison against the competition. We want your best creative thinking. Give yourself time to mull this over, go for a walk, or play some music. Let it noodle in your head. Think about your experiences with customers and your team. Think about what our business could be."

We ask leaders to bring their scratchpad of ideas to a strategy meeting. We tell them, "Don't try to come up with an NSP on your own, just work through the three questions as creatively as you can."

We typically work with senior leaders, and we also like to include some customer-facing people. When the group is together, we synthesize the information looking for themes and messages. We put people in groups to flesh out their answers to the three questions.

The three discovery questions serve three distinct purposes. First and foremost, within the group's answers is where you'll find your NSP. Secondly, the questions follow the model of appreciative inquiry. The act of asking and answering the questions prompts positive responses that stimulate people's frontal lobes. During the discussion, their brains release additional dopamine. This makes the group more engaged and creative. They bring their best selves to the process. Lastly, each question connects to what will later become elements of your strategy:

1. *How do you make a difference to your customers?* This defines your value to customers.
2. *How do you do it differently from your competition?* This establishes clear points of competitive differentiation.
3. *On your best day, what do you love about your job?* This provides the inspiration for emotional engagement.

We typically allocate a full day to creating an NSP and beginning to tease out the stories that will eventually prove it. Sometimes, we need to let the NSP sit for a bit and revisit it before we nail it down. In other instances, we've worked with groups over a series of conference calls. The critical elements in the process are that your NSP has to be informed by people who have direct experience with your customers. You have to allow the creative process time to work. And leadership must agree that it will become the lynchpin of your strategy.

Your NSP has to be specific and concrete enough to relate to your business, yet broad and inspirational enough to engage everyone. Without a clear NSP, you'll find yourself either being too vague or simply reverting back to the money story. Your NSP ensures that you and every member of your team has absolute clarity about how you make a difference in the lives of your customers. The following list includes NSP examples from 12 Noble Purpose firms that we've worked with. I've purposefully chosen clients from a variety of industries and of varying sizes to illustrate how the concept and methodology can apply to any business. In each of these firms, the words of the NSP are the jumping-off point for a strategy that cascades down to every level of the business.

1. **Blackbaud**
   We accelerate your Noble Purpose.
   Charleston, South Carolina, cloud company
2. **Commonwealth Assisted Living**
   We improve the lives of seniors, their families. And each other.
   Richmond, Virginia, chain of elder care communities
3. **Flight Centre**
   We care about delivering amazing travel experiences.
   Melbourne, Australia, travel firm with 22 brands
4. **G Adventures**
   We help people discover more passion, purpose, and happiness.
   Toronto, Canada, adventure travel company
5. **getAbstract**
   We turn employees into leaders.
   Miami, Florida, learning and development firm
6. **Hootsuite**
   We empower our clients to turn messages into meaningful relationships.
   Vancouver, Canada, SaaS company
7. **MMS**
   We help our customers save time and lives.
   Saint Louis, Missouri, medical distribution firm

8. **PharMEDium**
   We provide patient safety and advance peace of mind.
   Chicago Illinois, pharmacy sterile compounding firm

9. **Professional Women in Healthcare**
   We create leaders.
   National association of female healthcare leaders

10. **Porter Keadle Moore**
    We help clients seize opportunity and reduce risk.
    Atlanta, Georgia, accounting firm

11. **Explorys**
    We unlock the power of BIG DATA to improve healthcare for everyone Cleveland, Ohio, health care analytics

12. **Thomson Dehydrating**
    We make the world, and our customers, cleaner, safer, and more prosperous.
    Topeka, Kansas, manufacturing firm focused on growing renewable fuels

A Word about *We*

If you look at the previous statements, you'll notice that they all start with *We*. Companies are often tempted to shorten their NSPs to take out the word *we*, and start their statements with a verb instead. For example, Hootsuite's NSP would be, *Empowering our clients to turn messages into meaningful relationships*, and getAbstract's would be, *Turning employees into leaders*.

When I work with an organization to create their NSP, I always recommend starting the statement with *we*. In fact, I've become a bit of a stickler about it. I didn't used to be. An experience with one of my earliest purpose clients reveals why the word *we* is so important.

Graham-White is a Virginia-based company that makes compressed air drying technology and brake components for locomotives and rail transit markets.

Working with their leadership team, we created the NSP—*We make transportation safer, faster, and more reliable.* A few months later, I noticed they changed it on their signature line. It was now

Making transportation safer, faster, and more reliable. They'd dropped the *We*. The marketing department thought it read better without it. At first, I didn't think it was a problem. Yet over time, working with their people, I realized that dropping the *we*—two simple letters—had a big impact. Without *we*, it had become a tagline rather than a purpose statement. It was something they said, rather than something they did. It was a tagline, instead of the jumping-off point for strategy and behavior.

Fortunately, the leadership team agreed, and we changed it back to the original statement. I bring this to your attention because it's happened more than once. I now caution people about this in advance to make sure it doesn't happen.

The marketer in you (or your team) probably recognizes that it's a bit sexier and cleaner without *we*. I'm all for brevity, but in this case *we* is critical. Here's another example. Consider our client, getAbstract, the learning and development organization that produces, among other things, book abstracts. *Turning employees into leaders* is a brand promise. When the CEO Michel Koopman says, "*We turn employees into leaders,*" it becomes a behavioral mandate for every person in the organization. When a sales person is calling on a new client, her manager asks her before the call, "*How are you going to help this client turn their employees into leaders?*" When a developer is creating a new learning program, his goal is to turn more employees into better leaders faster. When the finance team is considering a policy change, they must think, *Will this help or hinder our ability to turn employees into leaders? Will it help people be better leaders, will it create more leaders?*

Taglines come and go, but your NSP is the guiding force of your business. It becomes your North Star, the aspirational aim that guides every element of your organizational strategy. The word *we* creates accountability and responsibility at every level of the organization. If you take *we* off, it's unclear who is supposed to be doing what. It erases accountability. *We* means the company; it's directly saying, "*Here is what we are here for.*" If you pull off *we*, there's no actor involved; there is no one initiating anything. So now whose responsibility is it? The statement seems more disposable. If it becomes a marketing message, it becomes a promise to the market, which may change as you develop new offerings. Taglines come and go. Your NSP is your unchanging strategy made manifest. It's the way your entire company lives. Everything is in service to it. It's your prime directive.

People get hopped up about sharing the NSP, but you have to bring your NSP to life internally before you can start sharing it externally. If you wind up using it publicly, great, but the primary purpose is to drive internal actions.

Your NSP is your North Star. An effective NSP:

- Describes your desired impact on customers
- Is a jumping-off point for strategy
- Defines expected behavior
- Provides a lens for decision-making

Your NSP should be short and concise. It should be written in plain language that you can describe to your kids or someone on an airplane. If you look at the NSP examples, you'll notice none of them describe products, nor do they describe specifics about the chosen customer base.

You need to know what you sell, and who you sell it to. But you don't need to include that in your NSP. Your NSP is about the impact you have on customers.

It will likely take you and your team a few tries before you come up with something everyone can agree upon. Don't short-circuit the process. And don't try to kitchen-sink it either. By that I mean don't try to throw in every single thing but the kitchen sink to appease every member of your group. Give it a few tries, and challenge yourself to be concise.

Once you've crafted your NSP, check it against these criteria:

- Is it short?
- Is it easy to understand?

- Is it concrete?
- Is it exciting?
- Can you explain it to your kids?
- Would you feel proud to share it with your neighbors?
- Does it make you want to get out of bed in the morning?
- Would you be proud for your customers to read it?

Once you've settled on your NSP, the next step is to share it with the rest of your organization. The process you use here is critical. We've outlined the steps in the Implementation Guide at the back of the book.

You'll want to use the three big discovery questions with every member of your organization. The people at other levels aren't going to be revising your NSP, but you do want them to own it.

People often ask, How does purpose fit in with mission and vision? How does it relate to your Why? Where do our values fit in?

Words only mean what we think they mean, so it's important to clarify. My favorite description of how purpose aligns with mission and vision comes from Roy Spence, in his book, *It's Not What You Sell, it's What You Stand For*. Spence writes:

Purpose is the difference you're trying to make.

Mission is how you do it.

Vision is how you see the world when you're done.

You can certainly have all three. But, as Spence says, "Purpose trumps everything." Many of our clients have had benign mission and vision statements that were already in place, mostly sitting on their website or on a dusty placard in their lobby. Rather than revisiting those, we simply moved on. We created a powerful NSP, and it stands by itself. The Noble Purpose is enough.

When we work with leaders on organization-wide implementations, we share the NSP as well as the process the senior team used to create it. Then we ask each department to unpack the questions for themselves. They need to be able to answer the three discovery questions from the vantage point their jobs and department: *How*

does your role make a difference? How do you do it differently from others?
On your best day, what do you love about your job?

This ignites their own emotional engagement. To be effective, every single person in your organization should be able to:

- Articulate your NSP.
- Share a customer-impact story that substantiates your NSP.
- Describe why it matters to them personally.

Remember, the purpose of the three big discovery questions is more than just crafting your NSP. They're designed to create an experience that enables people to internalize it and live it.

If you've done your job well here, people will be excited. Believe it or not, as a leader, your biggest challenge may be to direct their enthusiasm.

14

How to Keep Purpose from Being Hijacked

Leadership is the capacity to translate vision into reality.
—Warren Bennis

"This is perfect for our culture program," says the HR manager.

"We're going to use this as our new marketing campaign," adds the CMO.

"I can't wait for our social outreach team to use this in our philanthropy," says the Community Relations Manager.

These enthusiastic and well-intended comments can potentially be the death knell for your company's purpose. We've talked about what purpose is, and now it's time for us to talk about what it's not. Noble Purpose is not:

- A tagline
- A value proposition
- Servant leadership
- Customer-centricity
- Philanthropy
- A culture-building program
- A training initiative

These are natural *outcomes* of embracing a Noble Purpose philosophy and strategy, but there are distinct differences. A Noble Purpose
strategy will likely include all of the concepts in the list, but if you
allow it to be categorized as any one of these things, you run the
risk of it becoming siloed and marginalized.

Taglines Come and Go

The very nature of a great marketing campaign is that it's new and
fresh. Even the most successful campaigns rarely last more than a
year or two. Purpose, on the other hand, is constant. A good NSP
is inspirational and aspirational; there's also a bit of the plodder element present.

Since I originally wrote *Selling with Noble Purpose* in 2012, more
people are talking about purpose. There have been a number of
books on the subject, before mine, and after it. Yet I've noticed,
more often than not, that purpose is discussed in the context of
aspirational consumer brands and the messages they deliver to the
public. But purpose is not just for inspirational consumer brands.
While we love those kinds of brands, some of our most successful
clients are less public business-to-business organizations who have
held constant to their purpose for years.

If you allow your NSP to become a tagline, it's only a matter
of time before someone in marketing will want to change it. Make
sure that you've embedded your purpose into your operation before
you let marketing go public with it. Marketing should reflect your
purpose. It shouldn't become your purpose.

Beyond the Value Proposition

In most organizations, the value proposition typically sits in sales,
marketing, and service delivery. Noble Purpose organizations
have strong concrete value propositions with clearly differentiated
benefits. But your Noble Purpose is product-agnostic. It's activated

in every area of your organization. A strong value proposition is *part* of a Noble Purpose strategy. But it's not limited to customer-facing people or product production.

Customers and Employees Are Not Your Masters

Noble Purpose leaders have an ethos of service; they practice the tenets of servant leadership. Noble Purpose leaders are ambitious for their organizations, and their customers. While Noble Purpose leadership is about service, it's not servitude. Without a compelling cause, servant leadership can start to feel like indentured servitude. In a Noble Purpose organization, servant leadership is not the end game, customer-impact is. The tenets and behaviors of servant leadership are critical to helping a Noble Purpose leader lead. Noble Purpose leaders serve by taking people to new and better places. They rally their team in the service of their cause, the customer. Noble Purpose leadership ensures that everyone is in alignment around the same end game.

Cheryl Bachelder says, "Most people discount this as nice-guy leadership that's about hugs and campfires. Very few people have considered it might be the most effective. The greatest benefit is superior performance. Our goals are more aspirational, so the company is braver. We give dignity to human beings, and we attempt to be humble. People perform better under those conditions."

Customer-Centricity versus Customer-Impact

Noble Purpose organizations focus on their customers, but they go beyond customer-centricity. They focus on customer-impact. While it may seem like a nuance, this seemingly subtle difference in language creates a substantive difference in outcomes.

Henry Ford once famously said, "If I had asked them what they wanted, they would have said faster horses." Humanizing customers doesn't mean giving customers everything they ask for. Nor does it mean putting up with rudeness. And it certainly doesn't mean cutting the price. Organizations that embrace customer-centricity often find their people becoming reactive, responding to every customer demand. If a customer asks, it seems ignoble to say no.

Noble Purpose organizations don't reflexively give customers what they ask for. Instead, they point customers and their teams in the direction of what's possible. They prioritize based on where they can have the biggest impact, which can sometimes mean saying no to customer requests. Noble Purpose organizations have the courage to challenge and lead.

Commercial versus Philanthropic

Noble Purpose organizations tend to be generous. They're good corporate citizens. Organizations that focus on making a difference to customers create a big-hearted ethos. People in Noble Purpose organizations frequently volunteer their time. It's exciting, it's meaningful, it's wonderful, and, yes, it's noble.

But philanthropy is not the primary purpose of a Noble Purpose business strategy. I want to be absolutely clear about this: Noble Purpose is a capitalist, commercial model. It is about getting employees excited and engaged in the service of your customers. It is about creating competitive differentiation where it matters most. It's about doing work that matters and getting paid for it.

Philanthropy is a natural outcome of Noble Purpose; it's not the emphasis. When people first learn about Noble Purpose, their thoughts often naturally gravitate toward charity. When people say, "We should put our corporate responsibility team in charge of this," I know their purpose is at risk for descending into a feel-good, do-good sidebar.

Noble Purpose is a business strategy that applies to every aspect of the organization. After implementing Noble Purpose with hundreds of organizations, I've discovered that if you focus on philanthropy too early, people won't understand the commercial power. The most successful Noble Purpose organizations lead with the business case. Senior leaders own the initiative, not HR or community outreach.

Noble Purpose is about creating value; it's not giving away the store. I'm being emphatic about this, because I've seen it go the wrong way too often. When people hear "Noble Purpose," they often jump to giving away products to the needy, or doing volunteer work. These are great things, but they can't be the sole emphasis. When you diminish the commercial power of the concept, you ultimately erode your ability to be generous. Profitable organizations can do more good in the world than unprofitable organizations. They can be better employers and make better contributions to their communities.

Culture Follows Purpose, Not the Reverse

If you have a good HR and talent-development team, they're probably already working on your culture. Using your NSP as the lynchpin to drive culture will help them be more effective. But it's critical that they recognize two things:

1. Your NSP is not a culture initiative; it is a business strategy.
2. Your NSP alone will not create a culture.

A high-performance culture requires that you be explicit about your NSP and also your values. Effective cultures take time to create. Think about the example of the Thrashers at Foundation Supportworks, and the partners at Porter Keadle Moore, who took *yes, but* off the table. They were clear about their purpose. They also articulated their values and developed very specific processes and behaviors to ensure that their culture mirrored their aspirations.

Training Is Not Enough

A successful purpose initiative is going to involve training. But if you let your training department own the initiative, it will wind up becoming skills development rather than business strategy. It will be like the class in "Creating Effective PowerPoints." It's nice to learn, but if you have critical business, there's no real urgency to attend the session. Our most successful clients find that when senior leaders, particularly the CEO, own the initiative, they get immediate traction, and most importantly, better results.

Think about the CEOs you've met in this book. Mike Gianoni at Blackbaud, Skroo Turner at Flight Centre, Ryan Holmes at Hootsuite, Bruce Poon Tip at G Adventures, and Cheryl Bachelder at Popeyes. They live and breathe their purpose every day. They challenge their teams to think bigger on behalf of their customers. That's why their organizations get the results that they do. These leaders are master delegators, but they do not delegate their purpose.

Noble Purpose is an organization-wide strategy designed to improve competitive differentiation and employee engagement. It will make your business more profitable, and it will make your work and your team's work more meaningful. Your role as a leader is to harness your team's enthusiasm, without allowing your purpose to sit inside any one department alone. Invite your marketing, HR, and social responsibility teams to support the process. Build on their enthusiasm by giving them specific tasks to bring your purpose to life within their roles.

Cynics and Naysayers

We've covered the ways well-intended people can derail your purpose. At this point, we need to talk about the cynics. You probably already know who they are. From the eye rollers who sit in the back of the room, to subtle saboteurs who nod their heads in meetings then undermine your efforts after you leave.

For many years, the prevailing wisdom was that it's hard for people to change. But more recent change research reveals that people can actually change quite rapidly, if they know why the change is being requested. Change expert author Donna Brighton, who is President of the Global Association of Change Management, says, "True change cannot happen successfully without Noble Purpose. Whether it's personal change or organizational change, the heart of change is people. They need for change to be connected to a bigger why (Noble Purpose). People can deal with any change if there is a big enough why."

In our experience implementing Noble Purpose we find there are typical reasons people resist the concept:

1. They don't believe it's even possible.
2. They've never worked for anyone who thinks this way.
3. They don't believe their leader really means it.
4. Purpose is not aligned with their personal ethos.

If you encounter resistance, and you likely will, it's important that you give people space to come into the ideas on their own terms. One mistake we humans consistently make is expecting other people to match our thinking without giving them adequate time to process it.

Here's how it works. We hear an idea. We think about it for a while; we come back to it. We gradually assimilate it. Eventually it becomes our own. It feels as though we always thought that way. Then we enthusiastically share it with someone else; if they don't immediately mirror our enthusiasm, we're discouraged. We think, "This is such an obviously good concept. Why aren't they getting on board?" When we're invested in an idea, we often forget that it took us a while to get there.

Meet people where they are. For many people, this is a new way of thinking. It may be something they don't even think is possible.

Share the data about how purpose-driven companies outperform the market. Use the examples from the book to show your team what it looks like. Be willing to share the process you went through to get here. They need to see your authenticity.

People want to be part of something bigger than themselves. But how many of us have been burned in the past? We're all familiar with flavor-of-the-month initiatives. And let's be honest, at some point in our careers, many of us have worked for self-serving jerks who loved to give lip service to the newest management fads and trends.

Give your people time to understand why you're doing this. Let them know, it's not going away. Your consistency will make it clear: this is where we're going. Brighton says, "Leaders are great at starting things, they are not great at finishing things." It's the bright shiny object syndrome. We've all done it. But purpose is too critical to leave to change. Brighton says, "Instead of announcing 'here's the change, now you go implement it while I'm off to the next big thing,' great leaders stay with their teams through the process."

Setting crystal-clear expectations for your team is a tenet of effective leadership. If they're not the kind of people who want to be part of a larger purpose, they'll self-select out. This is a good thing.

People are looking for a leader they can believe in. That's why you can't be shy about sharing why this matters to you.

15

Why Your Backstory Matters

The best stories are often true. . . .
The narrative of human life is most beautiful when told truthfully and without boundaries.

—Shonda Rhimes,
creator and showrunner,
Grey's Anatomy and *Scandal*

Have you ever listened to a boring financial presentation?

Not to be dismissive of entire professions, but some groups have a reputation for being less than stellar storytellers. Full disclosure, my husband is a former finance guy.

If you find yourself on the giving or receiving end of a long, boring exposition, it's probably because the conversation focused on the front story instead of the backstory. To illustrate the importance of a compelling backstory, let's meet Milt, a financial planner. Like many personal finance experts, Milt gives free seminars to drum up business.

Milt has fairly decent attendance for his seminars. People show up, listen to Milt's advice, thank him, and leave. Milt offers a free personal assessment at the end, but very few people take him up on it. Milt needed more business, so he reached out to positioning expert Mark Levy to help him improve his presentation.

Levy asked Milt, "Why did you choose to become a financial planner?" Milt said, "When I was very young my parents passed away, and I went to live with my grandparents. They were great people, and I loved them dearly. They both worked at blue-collar jobs for the gas company, but they had always dreamed of owning their own business. One day, my grandmother saw an ad in the paper. A local hardware store was up for sale. When my grandfather came home, she showed it to him, saying, 'I think this is it. This is the business we've always dreamed about.' My grandfather agreed. They took their life savings and purchased the hardware store. The first year, they didn't make any money. The second year, they lost a little money. The third year, they lost all their money, and went out of business."

Their life savings was gone. They went back to their jobs at the gas company, where they both worked until they died. They never got to retire. They made a horrible mistake that cost them their golden years simply because they didn't have good financial advice. I decided that I didn't want that to happen to other people. So I became a financial planner."

Levy tells Milt, "The next time you give a seminar, I want you to tell that story before you start. Don't change any of your other content; just start the seminar by telling your backstory."

Milt began his next seminar saying, "I want to tell you why I became a financial planner." He spent three minutes telling the story about his grandparents. He then ran the seminar the same way he always did. At the end he made his usual offer for a free personal assessment. Every single person in the room signed up. Most of them wound up becoming clients.

What was the difference? How did one three-minute story take Milt from staid financial planner with a poor win rate to a compelling expert everyone in the room wanted to do business with?

Simple—once people knew Milt's backstory, why he was in his profession—the front story about how he worked became more authentic and compelling. Intent is always more interesting than implementation. As a leader, your team is always assessing your motives, consciously and unconsciously. If you want to get buy-in quickly, share your backstory.

Compare these two scenarios:

Julie Miller-Phipps is the newly appointed president of the Kaiser Permanente Health Plan in Atlanta, Georgia. In her previous position, she was senior vice president and executive director of Kaiser Foundation Hospitals and Health Plan in Orange County, California. She led a service area that has 23 medical offices and serves more than 480,000 members. During her career, she's opened two hospitals, she's worked as the Director of Hospital Operations, and she's been an assistant hospital administrator. She has a degree is sociology from Cal State.

Miller-Phipps had worked with Kaiser Permanente for more than 30 years. She has a long track record of success. As a hospital CEO, she has turned around unsuccessful hospitals. She's improved clinical outcomes. She says, "I've run hospitals where we started with patient satisfaction scores in the 25th percentile." Within two years of Miller-Phipps becoming CEO, patient satisfaction scores were at 95 percent, and she had less than 5 percent turnover. She improved accountability with everyone from the surgeons to house-keepers. She says, "My job as a CEO is to champion the vision and what it looks like in such a granular level that everyone can get it. And make it so compelling that people want to do it."

Imagine that Miller-Phipps is your new boss and she's just announced a quality improvement initiative. Do you believe she can do it? Are you motivated to bring your team into the process?

Given her background, you'll probably be pretty sure she can do it. But whether the project gets your time and attention remains to be seen. Quality improvement processes can be a long, slow grind.

Now let's put a new frame on the situation. You're meeting Julie Miller-Phipps for the first time. She's been introduced with the same impressive bio as above. But before she tells you about the change initiative, she tells you a bit about herself:

When I was a kid, I was always hyperactive. This was before ADHD was a diagnosis. I had a lot of energy. My mother was always looks for something for me to do. When I was 14, she got me signed up to be a candy striper at the hospital. I came home after the very first day and said, this is what I want to do with my life.

After high school, I went to nursing school. I was in year two of a four-year program, when my advisor told me I should work at a hospital over the summer to make sure this is what I really wanted to do. After the third year, when you do your clinicals, it's much harder to change your program.

I spent the summer at a hospital working alongside the nurses. Keep in mind, this was back in the 1970s. All the doctors were men, and many of them treated nurses badly. They were rude and disrespectful. I thought, *Okay, this is not going to work for me. I'm going to be fired within a week if I work here.* My 19-year-old brain said, *I'm going to quit nursing school, get a business degree, and run a hospital.*

That experience set the course for my life. I realized that we have to start with the belief that people are inherently good. No one wants to be perceived negatively. People want to have purpose in their lives. For me, a hospital is like an orchestra playing. You can watch moments of human connection happen. It's beautiful; it has profound impact.

I have a photo on my desk of myself as that 14-year-old candy striper. It reminds me that this is about reigniting people with the joy and passion for why they came into this business.

Now Julie announces that she's launching a quality improvement initiative. How motivated are you now? How willing are you to give it your time and attention?

Kaiser Permanente is our client. The above story isn't fictional; it's 100 percent true. Julie Miller-Phipps is the president of Kaiser

Georgia. You may have noticed that at the end of the second story, I called Miller-Phipps by her first name, Julie. Even though protocol dictates last names, it feels foreign. I can't bring myself to use it, because now I *know* her.

You probably feel the same way. We know why she's in this business and what her motivation is. When Julie tells you her backstory before she launches the quality initiative, you understand her intent, you know where she's coming from. As I said earlier, intent is always more interesting than implementation. That's why we tell our clients, *your why is always personal.*

Your team has to trust you before they'll fully support you. Julie's credentials command respect. Her backstory wins trust. When I enter her office on Piedmont Avenue in Atlanta, I see an impressive leader with a track record of success. When I see the photo of her as a 14-year-old candy striper on her desk, I see the ADHD kid who found her calling at the hospital. I would walk through fire for a leader like that. And so would most everyone else.

Your job as a leader is to speak to your team's best aspirations. People are complex; we each have good and bad within us; we have generosity and greed. It's easier, and more effective, to play to people's better natures.

We tend to judge ourselves based on our internal beliefs, our good intentions, and our highest aspirations. Yet we often judge others based on their external words and behavior. When you share your backstory with your team, you give them the opportunity to see your internal beliefs.

If you want an emotive response from others, you can't cloak your message in corporate speak. You have to be willing to bring your own humanity into the conversation.

Say What You Need to Say

I was working with the CEO of a pharmaceutical firm that specializes in allergy medicine. He'd just joined the company and was preparing for his first big Town Hall. As the new CEO, he recognized that people would want to know his plans. He prepared several slides about their position in the market, their opportunities, and his strategies.

I asked, "What do you want people to take away?" He said, "I want them to know the allergy business is important. We might not be curing cancer, but allergies affect people's lives."

"In what way?" I asked.

He said, "My wife has allergies. When they act up, it ruins family events for her. She had to leave our son's orchestra concert because she was wheezing so badly. She was so disappointed. She had been looking forward to it for weeks. People shouldn't have to suffer like that."

"Then why don't you just say *that*?" I asked.

He looked at me in disbelief, "Is it okay for me to talk about my wife's allergies?"

As the CEO, he felt that he should be professional, and just discuss business. In reality, his team wants to know who he is, and if he cares.

As we further explored, he said," I don't want to turn into a big mush ball in front of people. I don't want them to think I'm weird." Caring about your wife is hardly weird. Fortunately, this CEO is a smart guy. He quickly recognized the power of a personal emotive narrative.

He told the story about his wife's allergies at his Town Hall, and the reaction from his new team was overwhelmingly positive. They were thrilled to know that their new boss was emotionally invested in their products.

If you've been to business school, or had much corporate training, you're probably schooled in the language of corporate speak. Sometimes it's helpful. For example, distinguishing between strategy and tactics helps you formulate better plans. Knowing the difference between ideation and implementation enables you to clarify when to be creative and when it's time to be a taskmaster.

But in many cases, corporate speak removes you from the most important issues. People wind up overthinking things and watering down the most compelling part of their message. When you strip away the human element, you wind up losing the very thing that makes you engaging.

Why does this happen?

Discomfort with emotion is part of the problem. People are afraid to let things get too personal. This isn't just a problem in business. Too often, we cloak our most personal conversations with directives and commentary that cloud the true sentiment we need to convey.

For example, a friend of mine needed to have a difficult discussion with his 16-year-old son. He and his wife were divorcing, and my friend had decided that he was no longer going to be a member of the synagogue they had attended as a family.

My friend hadn't grown up Jewish. He was unchurched, meaning that he hadn't been raised with any type of religion. His wife was Jewish. When they got married, he agreed that the children should be raised Jewish. It wasn't a hard decision; he was happy for his children to have a religion in their lives.

Now, with the divorce process wrapping up, the temple asked if they would like to keep their family membership or split it. He decided that it just wasn't for him. But he was still committed to taking his kids. His challenge was how to tell his son, who was very committed to the Jewish faith. The divorce was hard enough for his son; my friend didn't want to make it worse.

He said, "I want my son to know that I'll still take him to temple. But I don't want him asking me why I'm not going anymore."

"What do you really want him to take away?" I asked.

He said, "I don't want him to think that I don't like his being Jewish. I'm glad he's Jewish. I'm glad my wife brought that into our family. I wish I had been raised with some kind of faith. I wish I felt as strongly about it as he does."

I asked, "Then why don't you just say *that*?"

It's a phrase I find myself using often with clients, and sometimes with myself.

When someone is struggling with a message, I ask, "What do you really want people to take away?"

The answer usually reveals a more direct and human message than their initial dressed-up version. The intentions behind the initial prepared offering is usually so much more clear and compelling that I find myself saying, "Why don't you just say *that*?"

Asking yourself, *What do I really want people to take away* shifts your mental process from thinking about your message to reflecting on the impact that you want your message to have. It enables you to become more personal, for yourself, and for the listener. You think more deeply.

Too often, we assume our intent is implied and the listener will infer our true message. It helps to define the words. When you imply, you hint at something rather than saying it directly. An implied meaning statement is hidden or folded into what was actually said. When a listener infers, she deduces meaning from what was left unsaid.

If the differentiation between the two words—imply and infer—seems unimportant or even silly, think about how senseless it is to rely upon these two techniques for communication.

My CEO client and my divorcing friend were leaving their true intentions unsaid. They were afraid that if they got personal, it would backfire. Too often, we cloak our personal feelings and direct our conversation toward the actions we want others to take. Yet the power of our own feelings is what will inspire others to take those actions. Your business conversations might not be quite as personal as my friends' conversation with his son. But they should have an emotional element.

Nothing bad happens when you let people know how deeply you care. When you say what you really want to say, you ignite a much better conversation.

You don't need to stifle your emotions, nor do you need to bleed all over the conference room. You just need to be willing to reveal something of your inner self, and not be afraid of a little vulnerability. As Brené Brown tells us, "Courage starts with showing up and letting ourselves be seen."

Ask yourself, *If I could say anything to these people, what would I tell them?* Your answer will reveal your true intent.

That's the conversation that your team needs you to have with them. People are looking for authentic leadership. You may not have a candy striper story in your background. You may not have had an epiphany while backpacking. But you probably have something. Maybe you're a scientist who loves chemicals, or an engineer who thinks making trains safer is the sexiest thing in the world. Think back: who were you when you were a kid? What did you want for yourself? That person is still inside you. Maybe you bounced around a lot before your found your place. Maybe you're still not sure what your future holds. That's okay. Your team just wants to know where you're coming from.

In the spirit of authenticity and vulnerability, here's some of my backstory.

I spent most of my high school years unhappy. To the outside world, I was a chatterbox, but on the inside, I felt that I didn't fit in. I felt I was on the sidelines, always watching, trying to figure out why people interacted with each other the way that they do, and why it seemed so easy for some and so hard for others.

In my first job as a salesperson for Procter & Gamble, I was thrilled to get the job. But after a few weeks, I realized I didn't like calling on grocery stores. It was the same thing every day, day in and day out. I was one of the few female sales reps out there, and the store managers were horrible. I gained 20 pounds in two years. I would come home at night, sit in front of the TV and drink wine and eat pizza with my husband. I faked it for 24 months, too stubborn to admit that the job might not be a good fit. Instead, I pretended that I loved my job, and did everything I could to get promoted. When I became a sales trainer, I realized that the way people interact with each other is the secret of everything. I loved it. I was mesmerized by the fact that a single interaction could change the entire course of human events. Sometimes, when I'm in the airport or at a party, I watch people and decode their interactions.

Over the course of my career, I've been fired from a waitress job and owned a business that went bankrupt. I've been the leader who'd lie awake on a Thursday night, staring at the ceiling, wondering how she's going to make payroll. I know that when you're not making money, you don't make good decisions. You're not a good boss; you're not a good parent. When you're worried about money all the time, you can't even function.

I've been a person who, at different points in my life, hated my job, and other times loved my job. I know that there's a big difference. When you hate your job, it has a chilling effect on your entire life. When you love your job it has a ripple affect on everyone around you. Your whole life lights up. Now, I'm a person who loves her job, almost everyday.

My purpose is to help people make money, and do work that makes them proud, because I know those two things change everything.

Think about yourself: how have your failures and setbacks contributed to who you are today? You needn't be embarrassed about them. They've brought you to where you are. In my experience, people who haven't ever failed at anything probably aren't trying very hard.

Your backstory doesn't have to be dramatic. It just needs to be authentic. If you grew up privileged, don't act as though you didn't. If you don't have a degree, don't be embarrassed about it. You are who you are.

Your team deserves to know who they're dealing with. They're trying to figure you out anyway, you might as well just tell them. People are sometimes reluctant to share their backstories and say what they really mean because:

- They don't fully understand it themselves.
- They think it's too personal and has no place in business.

- They think other people wouldn't buy into their motivation.
- They're afraid people will reject it.
- They're afraid people might confront them about it.
- They're afraid it will get out.

To this I must say, get over yourself. When leaders only share the fragmented, role-specific elements of themselves, their team is left guessing at the backstory. Or, more likely, they won't investigate. They'll make assumptions, or they just plain won't care. Sharing your backstory doesn't mean making it all about you. And it certainly doesn't mean reciting your résumé. Authentically sharing your backstory tells your team how you got here and why this matters to you. It establishes an environment of trust, which will help you get buy-in and make better decisions.

16

Give Yourself Space to Say No

The best time to plant a tree was 20 years ago.
The second best time is now.

—Chinese proverb

When CVS stores kicked their cigarette habit in October of 2014, they were making $2 billion a year selling tobacco. But they quit, cold turkey. They gave up $2 billion a year because selling tobacco was out of alignment with their true purpose. Their announcement read:

> Ending the sale of cigarettes and tobacco products at CVS/pharmacy is simply the right thing to do for the good of our customers and our company. The sale of tobacco products is inconsistent with our purpose—helping people on their path to better health.

In conjunction with the initiative, CVS renamed themselves CVS Health. They launched Let's Quit Together, a comprehensive personalized smoking cessation program to help their customers kick the habit as well. CVS President and CEO Larry Merlo said, "In quitting tobacco, we announced our plans to help

175

the 18 percent of Americans who smoke. We know that 7 in 10 smokers want to quit, so we've built a comprehensive national smoking cessation program that will help them do so."

How is CVS faring after giving up $2 billion in revenue?

Pretty well. They made headlines in every newspaper in the country. They've been lauded by medical professionals and business journals alike. Taking what seemed like a huge (short-term) hit to profits is actually going to help them make more money. Industry analysts believe that CVS will quickly replace their tobacco income with higher-profit smoking cessation and clinic services.

CVS's leaders didn't know they were going to launch a profitable smoking cessation campaign when they first started talking about giving up cigarettes. Their initial discussion likely focused on the disconnect between CVS's purpose, "Helping people on their path to better health," and the nicotine-laden death sticks they were selling at the register.

CVS had to decide what to stop doing before they could figure out what to start doing. When a leadership team identifies where they are out of alignment with their purpose, and has the courage to say, "We are willing to walk away from potential profits," the creative wheels begin to spin. In CVS's case, they came up with the Let's Quit Together campaign.

CVS had the courage to go first. They will reap the financial benefits of making their Noble Purpose the nexus of their business. If one of the competitors, Walgreens or one of the others, were to follow, they won't get the PR or revenue boost that CVS is getting. People will see Walgreen's as an also-ran, a company that only changed when the market was already moving. All the smokers who want to quit are already shopping at CVS.

Doing the Right Thing Makes You Money, If You Go First

It's never too late to do the right thing. But organizations who have the guts to go *first* have more firepower. The organizations that challenge long-standing business models on behalf of improving life for customers not only generate more goodwill, they have a strategic advantage because they create the new marketplace.

CVS was able to communicate the moral fiber of their company in a sweeping policy change that will improve the lives of their customers and ultimately make their organization more money.

CVS made headlines because they gave themselves permission to say no.

Steve Jobs famously said, "People think focus means saying yes to the thing you've got to focus on. It means saying no to the hundred other good ideas that there are. I'm actually as proud of the things we haven't done as the things I have done."

Saying no takes discipline. One reason leaders are reluctant to say no is because alternatives to the current model aren't always immediately obvious. Industry insiders say that CVS gave themselves time and space to come up with creative alternatives. Giving up their cigarette habit wasn't a quick decision.

As a leader, aligning your organization against your purpose will require saying no. Recognize that the space between when you say no and when you come up with something else may take a while. Give yourself some white space. Allow your team some time to think of creative alternatives.

Saying no may mean turning away business. It will definitely mean you don't go after every single market available. You'll say no to projects that might add value. You won't hire every person who has skills. You'll give up profitable lines of business. You won't go into markets where you could win deals. You'll shut down products that could potentially make you money.

If it sounds scary, that's because it is. But being clear about your purpose and your customer base will help you have the confidence to decide when to say yes and when to say no.

If CVS had a different purpose, they might have made a different decision. For example, their biggest competitor, Walgreens, has a different end game. According to Walgreen's website, Walgreen's vision is:

> To be America's most loved pharmacy-led health, well-being and beauty enterprise.

If your goal is to be loved, you're going to make different strategic choices. One could say that Walgreen's mission statement is customer-focused, but if you look closely, they're focused on the customer's response to them, not the customer's ultimate well-being. It's not a bad thing. I occasionally shop at Walgreens, and I like their stores. But CVS has a different purpose. CVS is about helping you on the path to better health.

Imagine that you're a smoker. You're out of cigarettes. It's raining, and you stop at the closest place to buy a pack. You've been buying cigarettes all your life, and you routinely buy them at drugstores. You don't even pay attention to which chain you're going into. Sadly for you, you've walked into a CVS. Right where the cigarettes used to be is a display for Let's Quit Together. Are you happy? Probably not. But CVS is not trying to be the most loved pharmacy; they're trying to help you on a path to better health. They were willing to anger some of their customers to do it.

If you're that smoker who needs a fix, you're going to turn around, get back into your car, and drive through the rain to Walgreens to buy your cigarettes. Their aim is to be the best loved, and in the moment you buy those cigarettes, you probably do love them. You love them dearly.

After they gave up cigarettes, CVS took it even further when they resigned from the U.S. Chamber of Commerce. On July 7, 2015, Reuters reported:

> CVS Health Corp said it was withdrawing its membership from the U.S. Chamber of Commerce after media reports that the trade group was lobbying globally against anti-smoking laws. The No. 2 U.S. drugstore chain said it was "surprised" to read recent reports on the chamber's position on tobacco products outside the United States.

The *New York Times* reported that the Chamber and its foreign affiliates were lobbying against anti-smoking laws such as restrictions on smoking in public places and bans on menthol and slim cigarettes, mainly in developing countries.

CVS spokesman David Palombi responded in an email statement:

> CVS's purpose is to help people on their path to better health, and we fundamentally believe tobacco use is in direct conflict with this purpose.

The Chamber said that it did not support smoking and called the report "a concerted misinformation campaign." In an email, the trade group said, "We support protecting the intellectual property and trademarks of all legal products in all industries and oppose singling out certain industries for discriminatory treatment."

The public skirmish will likely continue. But don't expect CVS to change their course. They're not afraid to say no to things that are out of alignment with their purpose. No matter what the cost.

Clarity of purpose won't make your decisions easy, but it will make them clear.

It's kind of like the monkey bars; you have to let go before you can move to the next rung. When you make the decision to say no, a new reality will eventually emerge. It may not emerge in the next five minutes, but it will come.

Bestselling author Marshall Goldsmith, who coaches some of America's top CEOs says, "People make poor decisions because they're attached to sunk cost."

You've probably experienced the emotional pull of sunk costs yourself. You've invested in the market or product line, but it's not working. But you can't pull out now, or all the money will be lost. You spent months looking for the perfect candidate, you invested time and money in their training. It's obvious that it's not working, but if you let him go, your investment will be lost.

Guess what? You've already lost your investment. Pulling the plug merely makes it official. As a Noble Purpose leader, you have to give yourself permission to say no to things that are outside your purpose. And you have to be willing to say no to things that aren't working.

It's hard to let go of something you're already invested in. But every minute you're wasting time on a mediocre situation is a minute you're not spending on the thing that might be your breakthrough.

Saying no to the wrong things enables you to say yes to the right things. Noble Purpose organizations don't shy away from Grand Challenges. A Grand Challenge is more than just a name, it's an official designation. WhiteHouse.gov provides a definition: "Grand Challenges are ambitious but achievable goals that harness science, technology, and innovation to solve important national or global problems, and that have the potential to capture the public's imagination."

Seth Kahan is an expert in Grand Challenges. Kahan is a Washington, DC–based consultant who works with top associations like the American Nursing Association and the American Geophysical Union to implement their Grand Challenges. When CVS kicked their cigarette habit Kahan wrote:

> With that one decision, they shifted their public identity one giant step toward becoming a trusted source of health and well-being, and an equally giant step away from being seen as a money-drive-all retail outlet. They were gambling on what every Grand Challenger knows; take bold, visible action toward the betterment of humanity and your organization will organically generate forward movement that includes: favorable public sentiment; advantageous new partners and stakeholders; media appearances that underscore your contributions to society; and of course, greater financial rewards in the medium-term, in exchange for a bit of cost up front.[1]

Once you have clarity of purpose, and have embedded it into your operation, you might consider taking on a Grand Challenge. It's something that is in alignment with your purpose, but it's a

---

[1]Seth Kahan, *Grand Challenges: The 7 Returns, and How CVS Changed EVERY-THING*, LinkedIn Pulse, June 22, 2015.

time-bound initiative that has a completion date. Kahan says that taking on a Grand Challenge often brings seven key returns:

1. *The business return*—Grand Challenges grow profitable revenue and other resources, which can be used for organizational wealth building.
2. *The mission return*—Grand Challenges amplify and scale your mission, improving your impact in both size and quality.
3. *The public sentiment return*—Grand Challenges dramatically improve public sentiment, garnering press and other visible accolades.
4. *The stakeholder return*—Grand Challenges attract new, powerful stakeholders aligned with your mission and goals.
5. *The engagement return*—Grand Challenges provide greater engagement for volunteer leaders and are exceptional for attracting next-gen-minded members.
6. *The relevance return*—Grand Challenges establish beyond the shadow of a doubt your organization's relevance to your members, potential members, and every beneficiary.
7. *The customer and member return*—Grand Challenges open up new career and learning opportunities, establishing new connections and expanding professional networks.

Kahan says, "Grand Challenges are by nature difficult to execute successfully—they are *grand*. There are many ways they can fail to provide on any or all of the above seven returns. But when executed well, a Grand Challenge is simply the most effective way to scale your impact and grow your resources." A Grand Challenge is a logical and powerful next step for a Noble Purpose organization. It requires a team that is not afraid to be bold and brave.

Don't Punish Errors of Enthusiasm

All mistakes are not equal, there's a big difference between errors of apathy and errors of enthusiasm. As every leader recognizes, your team is going to make mistakes. How you respond to those mistakes sets the tone for your organization.

Errors of apathy are the kind of mistakes that happened at GM. No one feels responsible, so everyone just passes the buck. Organizations run by quantitative metrics and productivity measures are more likely to create a culture where errors of apathy are tolerated, and tacitly encouraged. That's because the driving force is usually fear. People are afraid to make an error, so they don't challenge the status quo.

Errors of enthusiasm are driven by a desire for success. They occur when someone actually does something. They're born of hustle and innovation. They're more public. The consequences are more immediate, and the costs are obvious. Punishing errors of enthusiasm creates a climate where people are afraid to take risks. They're afraid to say yes, and they're afraid to say no.

In the early days of our business, money was tight. As our revenues grew, we loosened up the purse strings. One year, after we'd had our best year ever, we were reviewing the results. I noticed that my travel expenses were huge. I'd taken several fairly expensive trips that had not resulted in business. I told my husband, "Next year, I want to increase the win rate on these trips." He said, "I think that's a mistake. If some of your trips aren't working, you're not trying hard enough."

He was right; I wanted to be safe. I wanted every trip to pay off. But we'd just had our best year ever, in part because I'd been willing to get on an airplane when it wasn't a sure win.

You want your team to be smart about how they prioritize their time. But you don't want to hold them back because they're afraid of failing. Errors of apathy are driven by a fear of failure. The cost may not be immediately obvious; it's more insidious. People keep their heads down and follow the status quo. Over time, it winds up costing you more, due to lost opportunities.

As a Noble Purpose leader, your job is to take fear off the table. You need to help your team quiet their lizard brains. The lizard brain rears its ugly head when people are afraid. The reactive, fear-based, survival-at-all-costs amygdala makes people afraid to say no, even when something is outside your purpose. It prompts people to hold onto poor decisions because of sunk costs. It creates a climate where errors of apathy run rampant because people are afraid to take risks.

If you're going to be successful, you have to create the conditions that enable your team in making decisions with their frontal lobes. You have to prepare them in advance for difficult situations.

The Pre-Decision

People often agonize over noncritical decisions. Let's be honest, deciding what kind of car to buy is probably not going to have a big impact on your career or life. Yet people spend hours on that decision. And when it comes to deciding how you want to respond to stress, people often leave it to chance. But your behavior in critical situations is a decision, if not by design then by default. Being intentional about behavioral decisions is critical for you and your team.

Imagine your employee makes a significant error. Your response in the moment establishes the context for your future relationship. It will affect your employee's future performance, and it will affect everyone else on your team, because they'll hear about it. Your reaction will establish for your team that this is how the boss responds to errors.

Your reaction in high-stakes situations affects your success, your relationships, and over time, your reputation. Yet behavioral decisions are often made under stress, with no planning. In many cases, we often don't even recognize that it's a decision; we just react.

That's where the pre-decision comes in. The phrase was coined by our client, Kurtis Kammerer, Director of Sales Development for Foundation Supportworks, the Omaha, Nebraska–based construction company you met in earlier chapters.

Kammerer uses the technique to help his team make better decisions during times of stress. He teaches the technique by describing a situation with his son. He says, "I want my teenage son to start thinking of himself as a man who makes strong confident decisions, so I asked him, 'what kind of man are you? How would you describe yourself?' He described himself as an honest person, with high character and strong values. I said, 'Okay, great. Based on who you are, let's talk about what kind of decisions you want to make. We can predict what's going to happen. We know you're going to have someone offer you drugs. You're going to be with a young lady that you're very excited about. You're going to be in a situation where people are mistreating someone. We know in advance that all those things are going to happen. Let's decide now how you want to handle it, and write it down, so you will have already made the decision based on who you are.'"

Kammerer then draws a parallel for his team. He says, "We already know what's going to happen. You're going to drive up to a house that looks terrible. You are going to be at the end of the month, and you're not making your number. How are you going to respond?"

Kammerer tells new trainees, "There are going to be times when you don't like your company. It's all great now, you just joined. Every day is not going to be like this; there are going to be times, when you're mad at your boss. Based on who you are, how are you going to react? Let's decide now. Write it down."

The pre-decision model gives you and your team a tool for making decisions as your best selves, so when your worst day happens, you've already decided how you want to react.

Your business, and your life, are the sum of your decisions. There are times when you need to take a risk and say yes. And there are times when you need to give yourself the space to say no. You're going to make mistakes. That's a given.

When you stay true to yourself and your purpose, you stay pointed in the right direction.

17

Believe in the Dignity of Your Business

To be successful, the first thing to do is fall in love with your work.
—Sister Mary Lauretta

It's time for us to have an honest conversation about money. We've spent the majority of the book talking about how to shift the focus away from money. By this point, you understand that the money story is not nearly as powerful or sustainable as the meaning story. Companies with a Noble Purpose ultimately make more money because their teams are more engaged.

But let's be clear about the role that money plays in our businesses, in our own lives, and in the lives of our people. Money is important. Lack of money causes people to do all sorts of things.

I believe that business is a Noble Endeavor and that you deserve to be paid for it.

Shifting your focus from profit to purpose is not about making less money. It's a mistake to interpret it as such.

Our society sends us a polarizing message about money. We've heard that money is the root of all evil. We grew up with the story of miserly Ebenezer Scrooge keeping Bob Cratchit's family in poverty.

We love to hate Homer Simpson's boss, the evil Mr. Burns, the owner of the Springfield Nuclear Power Plant, who cackles as he poisons his community to make an extra buck.

Yet we know that not having money makes it hard to live your life. We enjoy the things that money can buy for us and our family. If you're reading this book, odds are at some point you've enjoyed the benefits of a nice meal or vacation.

Is money bad, or is money good? I come down on the side of good. In one of my favorite books about money, *Thou Shall Prosper*,[1] Rabbi Daniel Lapin says, "Believe in the dignity and morality of your business."

Rabbi Lapin shares a great lesson from economic professor, Walter Williams, who says:

> Take out a dollar bill and look at it. Now pat yourself on your back because you are looking at a certificate of performance. If you did not rob or steal from anyone to obtain that dollar, if you neither defrauded anyone nor persuaded your government to seize it from a fellow citizen and give it to you, then you could only have obtained that dollar in one other way—you must have pleased someone else.

Rabbi Lapin writes, "How true are those words. Whether you pleased a client, a customer, or your boss, that money is a testament to your having pleased another human being. Having money is not shameful, it is a certificate of good performance granted to you by your grateful fellow citizens."

As a Noble Purpose leader, you must believe that your business adds value to the world, and that you deserve to be paid for it.

I haven't always been as declarative about the nobility of business as I am today. For many years, I felt a push-pull between doing good and doing well. I've always been a very ambitious person.

---

[1]Rabbi Daniel Lapin, *Thou Shall Prosper: Ten Commandments for Making Money* (Hoboken, NJ: John Wiley & Sons, 2010).

Yet at times I felt as though my work wasn't as noble as being a teacher, social worker, or a surgeon. It took a trip to China for me to fully internalize just how critical capitalism is for a prosperous and healthy society.

The Moment I Fell in Love with Capitalism

I was visiting China a few years ago with my oldest daughter. We were with a tour group, but we had some time to explore on our own. We ventured slightly off the beaten path. We found ourselves walking the back streets on the outskirts of a village situated amongst several canals.

Keep in mind, China is (relatively) recently emerging from being a Third World country. There's still plenty of poverty. During the trip, we'd seen a mix of upscale and impoverished areas. The canals and village we were walking alongside were somewhere in between. They were beautiful. But they weren't like canals in Venice or Vienna, lined with cafes and hotels. These were working canals, lined with small one- and two-room wood and stucco homes that sat flush up against the canals. The homes didn't have running water. People were doing their wash in the canal, leaving it to dry on makeshift clotheslines or laid out on rocks.

I'm always interested in how people live their daily lives. A long, slow walk through a residential area in another country gives you an opportunity to observe daily life in a way that you can't see from a tour bus or hotel balcony.

The homes along the canals were jammed in one right next to the other, sharing common walls. The exteriors all looked very much the same. The backs of the homes were to the canal. The front doors opened right onto the dirt street, with no yard or buffer zone between the homes and the street.

As we walked, I began to notice the floors inside the homes. As the locals went about their business, going in and out of their homes, opening and closing their doors, I could see that most of the homes had dirt floors. But a few had tile floors, relatively new looking shiny tile floors.

Walking further, I noticed that the people with dirt floors opened and closed their doors quickly, getting in and out fast, with their heads down, as if to avoid letting anyone see inside their homes. The people with tile floors swung their doors open wide. Many of them were selling things like hand-carved wood pieces or fans. Some had single chair beauty parlors and barbershops in their front rooms.

Ever the businessperson, and also a home improvement junkie, I said to my daughter, "I would love to be a tile salesperson here!" As we walked, we mapped out our imagined marketing plan. We'd take a wagon of shiny tile up and down the street, offering next-day installation. We'd offer a few key opinion leaders great deals, if they agreed to leave their doors open during the day. We'd approach the barber and beauty shops and tile their spaces for free if they let us set up marketing displays. Within two blocks, we had created our tile empire.

As we were planning our three-village expansion plan, we came upon the local home improvement warehouse. We quickly saw that we weren't the only people to recognize the great opportunity in flooring tiles.

Picture a metal building about as big as a two-car carport. The roof is 15 feet off the ground. One side of the building is completely open to the outdoors. The building is filled with metal shelving units crammed with light fixtures, hardware, lumber, and loads of tile.

Lined up around the open side of the store are 15 or 20 three-wheel scooters with small flatbeds on the backs of them. These belong to the Chinese contractors, small, slim, fast-moving men, pushing their way in and out of the skinny aisles buying supplies. They're grabbing materials right and left, hurriedly paying for them, and loading them onto their flatbeds before they zoom off down a side street. Almost every load includes a box of tile.

There was an energy in that home improvement store that we hadn't seen in the poorer areas. It was vibrant and alive. The contractors were buying things and selling them. They were making money, they were improving their own lives, and they're helping people improve their homes.

That's when it struck me; the difference between the home-owners with their doors that were wide open, and those who shuffled in and out quickly keeping their doors shut was pride.

The people who had improved their homes were proud of what they'd done. Other parts of China had felt grim and hopeless. But in that village, the energy of commerce was starting to emerge. The home improvement store was buzzing. It was alive with people taking control of their own destinies.

At that moment, any ambiguity I had about capitalism was gone. Making money and putting money into motion creates energy. Those Chinese tile contractors were engaged in a noble cause. So were the people selling things to tourists and doing hair. They were bringing the energy of commerce to their people.

The beauty of capitalism is that it gives people the power to control their own destiny and to add value to the lives of others.

It's easy to say that people don't need more stuff. In my part of the world, many of my peers are trying to reduce their material possessions rather than add to them. But we don't have to raise our families in two rooms with dirt floors. The fact is, capitalism is the best, most sustainable way to lift people out of poverty.

Sure, some people have abused capitalism. People have also abused families. But no one ever suggests that families themselves are the problem. Human endeavors will always be fraught with errors.

Capitalists often get a bad rap. The story of the greedy immoral businessperson is a common pop culture narrative, a staple of movies and TV shows. Cut to the evil businessman, cackling as he counts his coins while his workers slave away in the salt mines, giving their lifeblood for his riches.

We've all seen that story. But that's not the whole story. The larger story is this:

Prior to the Industrial Revolution, most of the world lived in poverty. According to research from the World Bank[2] on the year 1000, real GDP per capita was $435 per year (in today's dollars); 750 years later, in 1750, it was only $667. During the first few thousand years of our existence, for most humans, life was sheer survival. People spent their days scrounging for food and seeking shelter. Very few lived past forty.

In the 150 years after the Industrial Revolution, real GDP rose to $2,113 and by 2013 it was $13,100.

That's capitalism in action. Can you envision any way that humanity could have advanced from scrounging for food to building art museums without capitalism?

Many people on the planet are still in survival mode, but that's not *because* of business. It's the *absence* of commerce that keeps people impoverished.

Conscious Capitalism's Raj Sisodia,[3] whom you met earlier when he described lack of employee engagement as like a rowing scull with two people beating the others over the head, says, "Capitalism is ending poverty on Earth."

As for the claim that business is unethical? I side with Sisodia, who says, "Business is inherently ethical because it is based on a voluntary exchange."

Envision a thriving society where people have the capacity to care for their families, and spend their days making meaningful contributions. Can you imagine that world existing without free enterprise? Of course not, a thriving community depends upon people buying and selling their wares in a free market.

---

[2]Raj Sisodia, David Wolfe, Jag Seth, *Firms of Endearment: How World-Class Companies PROFIT from Passion and Purpose* (Upper Saddle River, NJ: Pearson Education, 2014).

[3]Raj Sisodia, Public Comments Conscious Capitalism Conference, Chicago, April 18, 2015.

People can only thrive when they take control of their own economic futures and they have the capacity to buy goods and services to improve their lives. Yet despite solid evidence that capitalism lifts society, cynicism and distrust in business have increased in recent years.

It's because we've let a few greedy, self-serving fools define the narrative. We look at a hedge fund manager who acts unethically or a CEO who makes 400 times his average worker's salary. We forget about CEOs like Kip Tindell, of The Container Store, who makes at most 35 times the average store worker. Tindell says, "CEOs are important, but not as important as they're made out to be." Not surprisingly, for the last 15 years The Container Store has been on *Fortune* magazine's list of "100 Best Companies To Work For."

We make movies about greedy investment bankers while real-life leaders like Bob Chapman, Chairman and CEO of Barry-Wehmiller Companies, a $2 billion global organization, achieve a 20 percent compound growth rate over 20 years by focusing on "Truly Human Leadership." Chapman's principles include: "Look for the goodness in people, and ask no more or less of anyone than you would of your own child."

We've seen through the work of Wharton Professor Adam Grant and others that people who bring a generous spirit to business are more successful for themselves and their organizations over the long run. In his book *Give and Take*, Grant's research reveals that people who take an I-win *and* you-win approach create more value than those who view the people on the other side of the negotiating table as an adversary.

Believing in the dignity of your own business also means believing in the dignity of everyone else's business. It's worth saying something here about vendors. Citing the work of Ruth Blatt,[4] in her *Academy of Management Review* paper about the complex interplay

---

[4] Adam Grant, *Give and Take: A Revolutionary Approach to Success* (New York: Viking, 2013).

between relationships and contracting, Grant says, "I've seen over and over again, people making the mistake of running to contracting too soon, before the relationship is solidified and strengthened. When people impose bureaucracy and red tape, it can destroy relationships and undermine the value."[5]

Noble Purpose leaders don't beat up their suppliers. Grant says, "My goal is not to get people to start giving so they can get ahead, my goal is to take people who already want to give and show them that it does not have to hurt your career."

The takers are not the norm. It's time to stop letting a few high-profile outliers define the story of business. Noble Purpose is about harnessing the power of capitalism to do great and amazing things.

Now I'm going to say something that may seem to fly in the face of what I've said thus far: part of your job as a Noble Purpose leader is to help your people make more money.

Why is that a noble cause? Because sometimes people need help seeing what's possible.

I was working with a client whose salespeople sold to individual homeowners. The salespeople were on commission. Most made between $50,000 and $60,000 per year, but some made $70,000 or $80,000. The difference in commissions wasn't due to any differences in territories; the people making more had simply set their bars higher. The CEO said, "I wish I could get these other guys to see that they could be making more money." Most of the salespeople lived in small towns, and a lot of them had grown up blue collar. Most of them were making about the same money as the people they grew up with. In a small town, you can have a pretty decent life on $50,000 a year.

The CEO loved his team. But he knew that many of them struggled with money. You can have a decent life on $50,000 a

---

[5]Ruth Blatt, *Tough Love: How Communal Schemas and Contracting Practices Build Relational Capital in Entrepreneurial Teams* (Academy of Management Review, July 2009).

year, but it's going to be tough to send your kids to college. He knew that the salespeople making $20,000 or $30,000 a year more weren't working longer hours. They had set different expectations for themselves, and within a normal amount of hours, they aligned their behaviors to meet their goals.

The CEO didn't want to stand in front of his team and say, "Hey guys, you could be making more money." He'd tried that and it hadn't worked.

Instead, we created a side-by-side chart.

On one side was the salesperson who made 10 sales calls a week, and closed two deals. On the other side was a salesperson who made 12 calls a week and closed three deals.

The salesperson who closed two deals a week helped 100 customers this year. The salesperson who closed three deals a week helped 150 customers.

The salesperson who closed two deals a week made $50,000. The salesperson who closed three deals a week made $75,000.

The difference was $25,000 of income. But what did that really mean? Telling people they could make $25,000 a year more isn't very inspiring if they've never really thought about what it might mean for them.

The salespeople were primarily men in their mid-thirties with young families. So the CEO framed the money around things he knew were most important to them. He said, "Here's a guy who makes $25,000 more, over 10 years; that's two paid-for college educations. That's the difference between your kids coming out of school saddled with debt or you being able to send them to their dream school, and them having a free and clear education. That's a lake house for your family that you can enjoy for generations. That's you being able to give money to your church or community."

As a Noble Purpose leader, if you want the best for your team, you need to have an honest conversation with your people about money. Showing them what's possible doesn't mean you expect them to sacrifice their lives at the altar of the bottom line. It simply means you care about them enough to help them dream big dreams.

They can choose whether or not they want to go after them. As a leader, it's your job to show them that they are available.

I believe in pay for performance. I believe that it's okay to be rich. We know some rich people are wonderful and add value to the world, while others are takers with little regard for their fellow man. Greed is not good, neither is entitlement. But wanting to make money for bringing value to others is not a bad thing. It's a natural aspiration for most human beings. For me, the secret to a good mental relationship with money comes down to four things:

1. Be grateful for what you have.
2. Believe in your value.
3. Charge what you're worth.
4. Be generous.

Peter Drucker once said, "Profit is not the purpose of a business, it's the test of its validity." Making money and making meaning are not in conflict. They are inextricably linked. When you make the wheels of commerce spin, you put human energy into motion.

18

The DNA of a Noble Purpose Leader

Purpose is like a plant. You have to water it, you have to tend to it, you have to nurture it.

—Bruce Poon Tip, Founder, G Adventures

In business, we've been dancing around purpose for decades. It's evolved. Some of the earlier versions include:

- Reputation—When businesses were more local entities, owners cared about their reputations.
- Motivation—As owners recognized the importance of employees, they tried to improve results by using money internally for employees.
- Competitive Advantage—As business became more sophisticated, organizations showcased their differentiators and customer benefits externally.

People have also used words like *customer-focus* and *attitude*. We now recognize that those earlier concepts are the behaviors and outcomes that stem from the right purpose.

But a purpose is only as good as the leader who champions it. In today's fragmented, 140-character, everything-right-now environment, leadership is everything. Leadership is distinguishing the differences between organizations that succeed and those that fail.

By now, you recognize that as a leader, you're the lynchpin. If your organization is going to rise above mediocrity, you have to be the one who takes it there. Here's a summary of what's required to become a Noble Purpose leader:

Have Absolute Clarity about Your NSP

Noble Purpose leaders are absolutely explicit about their NSP; it's the gestalt of their business, the centerpiece of their strategy. They have complete clarity about how they make a difference to their customers. And they repeat it over and over again, using compelling stories to demonstrate their focus and commitment to their NSP. For them, the big win isn't just hitting the numbers or beating a competitor; it's the impact they have on customers. They create competitive differentiation because they know exactly how their organization improves the lives of customers, and how they do it differently from anyone else. And they make sure every member of their team knows as well. Their entire organization aligned to achieve their NSP. When they talk about their business, they glow with pride as they tell stories about their customers.

Use Customer-Impact Metrics

Noble Purpose leaders understand that today's numbers are the result of the human interactions, attitudes, and behaviors that occurred months earlier. They go beyond standard metrics to continually ask, "How well are we performing against our purpose?" They look for creative ways to measure customer impact. They read what customers write on their comment cards. They actively seek out users, and non-users, to get candid feedback. They listen to sidebar conversations. They read the employee engagement surveys and they go on Glass Door to read the unfiltered comments.

They manage the creative tension between profit, process, people, promotion, and products by keeping purpose at the fore. They dig behind the numbers to understand what's really happening on the front lines.

Rally Your Team for the Cause Called Customers

Noble Purpose leaders are intentional about creating a culture that is on fire for customers. They know who their customers are and who they are not. They meet with customers and users on a regular basis. They invite customers to their meetings. They put photos of customers on their walls; they have dance parties when they get a big win. They tell customer-impact stories every chance they get. They organize their entire organization around helping their customers succeed.

Believe in the Dignity of Your Business

Noble Purpose leaders understand that making money and making a difference are congruent. They know their products and services make a difference in the lives of their customers, and they're not afraid to charge accordingly. They don't play price wars, and they don't belittle their vendors. They create value for everyone. Noble Purpose leaders make a point to help their people achieve financial success. They believe in pay for performance. They know that money is a tool to make people's lives better. They're generous with their team and their community.

Give Yourself the Space to Say No

Noble Purpose leaders don't try to please everyone. They're not afraid to say no. They don't let sunk costs of the past determine their direction for the future. They're willing to let go of a market or a customer base, if it's out of alignment with their purpose. They're also willing to take on grand, sometimes seemingly impossible challenges, if they believe that they will make a difference to their constituents. They don't succumb to false dichotomies. They continually ask, Where is our best and highest use? Where can we do the most good, in the biggest, boldest ways?

Stay Resilient

Noble Purpose leaders live their Noble Purpose on their best days, and on their worst days. They're not easily derailed in the face of adversity. They're realistic optimists who aren't afraid to confront the facts, and make difficult decisions. Noble Purpose leaders know that failure is always temporary. They don't overreact. They use constancy of purpose (and humor) to bounce back from setbacks and mistakes. They're not afraid to get help, or admit mistakes and losses.

Be All In

Noble Purpose leaders don't shy away from emotion. They love their job, they love their customers, and they love their team. And they're not afraid to let everyone know it. For them, business is personal. They don't shy away from difficult conversations. They care enough to address the tough stuff, head on. They give direct feedback. Noble Purpose leaders are attuned to the emotional undercurrents of their organization. They're not perfect, but their team knows their passion comes from their belief in a cause bigger than themselves.

Above all, in good times and bad, Noble Purpose leaders know their work matters. They build a tribe of True Believers because they're all in.

Here's a snapshot of what makes a Noble Purpose leader different:

	Mediocre Leaders	**Noble Purpose leaders**
Belief	Mediocre leaders view the organization as a cash register; pulling the right levers produces wealth for the owners.	Noble Purpose leaders care passionately about the impact business has in the world; they love their industry, their team, their users, and their customers.
Measurements	Define success through internal metrics.	Define success through customer-impact.
Decision-making	Make reactionary decisions, based on the competition, short-term profits, and sunk costs.	Make strategic, often gutsy, long-term decisions based on values and purpose.
Language	Use corporate speak and non-emotive language.	Share their personal backstories and aren't afraid to get emotional.

A recent *Forbes* article revealed that 65 percent of people would rather have a different boss than a raise. I hope you'll use this book to ensure that your team doesn't become part of that 65 percent. The information you've read thus far and the Implementation Guide on the following pages have set you up for success. The rest is up to you.

I started off this book talking about my father. In many ways, this book is a testament to him, to the life he led, and the leadership he displayed as a businessperson, public servant, and father. It's also more than that. It's a call for today's leaders to become the kind of leaders who are worth following.

When I was 25 years old, my father shared something with me that forever altered my perspective on leadership. I had just been promoted to my first manager position at Procter & Gamble. I called my father to give him the good news. "Congratulations," he said,

"You've just become the second most important person in the lives of your employees." "What do you mean?" I asked. He explained, "Next to your spouse, your boss has the most power to make your life wonderful or miserable."

At the time, his comment petrified me. I was only 25, half my team was twice my age. I was scared to death because I knew my father was right. Think about your bosses and the impact they've had on you. If you're the boss, you're a looming presence in the lives of your people, whether you like it or not. You have the power to create happiness, or misery.

After my father passed away, I found myself missing him more deeply than I'd ever missed anyone. I wasn't alone. One former colleague, who hadn't seen my father for 20 years, said, "When I found out Jay died, I burst into tears."

I came to realize the reason I, and so many others, felt the loss so deeply wasn't just because of the things my father did; it was the way he made us feel. As the late Maya Angelou said, "I've learned that people will forget what you said. People will forget what you did. But people will never forget the way you made them feel."

You've probably learned the same thing yourself. The people you miss the most are the people who make you feel like you matter.

You have the power to make your team feel like they matter. As a leader, you're the one who tells your people whether this is just a job, or whether their work actually counts for something.

Your career may seem like a long journey, but eventually it's going to be over. At some point, you're going to be the one in the hospital bed reflecting on what it all really meant. At that point, all you have left is your legacy.

You can be the leader whose team experienced their work as just a grind. Or you can be the leader whose people say, "I burst into tears when I heard he died."

The choice is yours.

PART II

Implementation Guide for Noble Purpose Leaders

Efforts and courage are not enough without purpose and direction.
—John F. Kennedy

19 | Claim Your Noble Purpose

What follows is the process we use for large-scale purpose implementations. If your team is smaller, the process works the same way. You simply have fewer players involved. The process is somewhat fluid. The phases go in order, but they bleed into each other, rather than standing alone. This guide may seem daunting at first. It needn't be. You can do this. Each element is spelled out in simple terms, and quite honestly, you don't have to do it all perfectly. Just stay the course and keep doing it.

In this phase, you'll identify your aspirations for your clients, what your competitive differentiators are, and what ignites emotional engagement for yourself and your team. It's crucial that you get input from senior leaders and customer-facing employees including sales, service, and delivery people. In this phase, you want to investigate the impact your products and services can have on customers. It's critical that you get beyond generic features and benefits. This phase is meant to be both inspirational and accurate.

Answer the Three Big Discovery Questions

This is a robust conversation with your team. The three discovery questions (below) require time and exploration.

If possible, it's also worth exploring these questions with your customers. We typically assign the three questions as a pre-work activity for a group session. An ideal group to explore the discovery questions and craft your NSP would include senior leaders and a cross-section of top-performing field sales, service,

Stop!

Stay away from corporate speak. This doesn't need to be vetted by engineering or legal; it's anecdotal at this point.

and operations people. When you assign the three questions, make it clear that this is a creative brainstorming exercise that will inform the next phase. Your people can use stories, examples, and personal reflections to answer the questions.

How do you make a difference?	*How do you do it differently than your competition?*	*On your best day—what do you love about your job?*
Think about how your products and services affect customers' lives and businesses. Go beyond simple things like "we make their processes faster" or "we help them improve their systems." Think deeply about the larger implications. Do you help them sleep better at night? Do you help them make better decisions? Your products and services don't have to be exclusively responsible for these things, they just have to contribute.	You may have some technical advantages. In addition to product differentiators, think about how doing business with you and your team is different than your competitors. Do you care more? Are you more fun? Do you provide deeper expertise? What you're looking for here is both tangible and intangible ways that you stand out.	This is highly personal for each person. What you're looking for here is an emotive response. Think about the days when, at the end of the day, you said "this was a great day." What made it so?

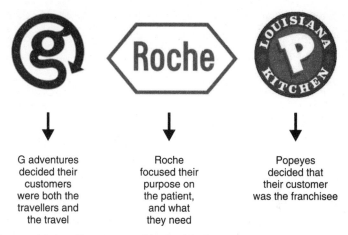

| G adventures decided their customers were both the travellers and the travel | Roche focused their purpose on the patient, and what they need | Popeyes decided that their customer was the franchisee |

Figure 19.1   Customer Clarity Drives Focus

Get Clarity on Your Customers

Before you can craft your NSP, you need to clarify exactly who your customers are, and who they are not. Are they the end users? Or are they the resellers? You must be specific. Remember these examples? (See Figure 19.1.)

Don't make the common mistake of believing that you can serve everyone. Trying to serve multiple masters waters down your NSP. Your customer must be someone who is directly connected to the revenue chain of your business. They either buy or recommend. Your customer is not the shareholder or internal stakeholder.

Declare Your NSP

This is a creative process best done as a facilitated group exercise. We typically do this in a one-day strategy session, where we also tackle some items in Phase 2. We have each member of the team describe their answers to the three big discovery questions. We look for themes and commonalities. We make a list of the words that we continue to hear. We often use a word cloud as a tool. We do multiple passes at crafting a succinct, compelling NSP. As a reminder, here are some samples:

- Hootsuite
  We empower our clients to turn messages into meaningful relationships.
- Commonwealth Assisted Living
  We improve the lives of seniors, their families. And each other.
- Flight Centre
  We care about delivering amazing travel experiences.

Why these work:

These NSPs are the result of robust discussions framed around the three discovery questions with groups of high performers. They speak to their aspirations for clients. They can be translated into behaviors for every single member of the organization. They act as the North Star for strategy.

Stop!

Don't try to crowbar your products or services into your NSP.

Now that you have your NSP, you're ready to create the story around it.

20

Prove Your Noble Purpose

If you want to get immediate traction, you'll need to do more than simply share your NSP. You need to prove it. This phase is about concrete substantiation. This is where you'll codify the stories to substantiate your NSP and identify a few immediate actions to demonstrate your commitment. This additional preparation lets your team know that this is more than a flavor-of-the month tagline. Engage the most senior leader possible, ideally the CEO. You should also engage peers and your direct reports. You want their support before you launch your initiative broadly.

Create the Narrative

Your NSP takes what is implicit in your business and makes it explicit. To bring it to life, you need compelling customer-impact stories. Customer-impact stories demonstrate what living your

NSP looks like in practice. They provide proof that you and your business can deliver on your NSP. At this point, you don't have to be living your NSP perfectly. Compelling stories will show your people what's possible and challenge them to bring your NSP to life in bigger, bolder ways.

Many of these stories likely emerged when you explored the three discovery questions. Take the time now to bring them to life with a narrative and visuals in preparation for your launch. A large firm might create an emotive video; a smaller firm could share photographs of clients. You'll

Stop!
Ask yourself—How do I feel telling this story? That will be a clear indication if the story is boring or inspiring.

also want to look for additional sources for stories. For example, one of our pharmaceutical clients found several public stories in a patient-support group blog. At this point, you're collecting stories to be told internally. They should be true, but they don't have to be vetted for public use yet. These are not pitches filled with product information. These are stories about how you made a difference to customers. They need to be exciting, interesting, and emotional. Ask yourself, *Would I want to listen to this?*

Note—A customer-impact story is not a traditional case study. Most case studies are a fact-based retelling focused on product features and implementation. That's hardly the stuff that moves hearts and minds. Traditional case studies, or descriptions about how you beat the competition and won the business, do not connect to your NSP. Instead, combine facts with emotion to illustrate the impact you had on an individual customer.

These stories will be the lynchpin of your launch; they're what your team will remember the most. You want to craft stories that will be easy to share with their spouses and children. Your stories will illustrate that your company does more than just make money; you also make a difference. And you're going to start living your NSP in even bigger, bolder ways.

Personalize It

Stop!

Are you showing your true self, or are you trying to integrate your products? Open your heart. Why are you here?

It's crucial that you, the leader, have a personal connection to your purpose. This is where you create your back-story. Think about why this matters to you. Do you want people to experience the wonders of travel because it has had such a profound effect on your own life? Are you driven to make things safer because you once saw a bad accident? Do you want to cure disease because you've seen the tragedy of human suffering? Your team is going to want to know why this matters to you personally. Launching a Noble Purpose initiative isn't about you; it's about your customers. Sharing your personal connection to the purpose tells your team why you care. Don't shy away from opening yourself up. Your backstory should be *authentic, organized*, and *true*.

Identify your Acclerators

Stop!

Do not pick something that requires a lot of time and resources. This needs to be a quick win for you.

Before you launch your Noble Purpose initiative publicly, you and your team should identify some quick wins. These are your Noble Purpose Accelerators. They're the immediate action items that you'll announce during your launch. They demonstrate that you are already operationalizing your purpose.

An Accelerator might be a small change in policy like extending service times. It might be changing your meeting format to discuss customer-impact stories for the first five minutes, instead of financials. It might be including the client mission on the front end of your sales presentation templates. It might be a new training program or launching a story contest. Working with your team, choose something that will be positively received and easy to implement immediately.

Purpose Accelerator Checklist

- Will this give you a quick win?
- Does it move the narrative toward customers?
- Does it make less work for people?
- Is it in alignment with your NSP?
- Is it easily understood?
- Is it popular, and will people like it?
- Do you have the authority?
- Can you implement immediately?

The Accelerators will give you traction and leverage. These should not be complex or difficult; you'll tackle harder challenges later. These are kick-starters you'll use during the launch phase. Choose at least one, but no more than three.

Now you've proven your NSP with customer-impact stories. You've thought about your personal backstory, and why this matters to you. And you've chosen the Accelerators that will give you some quick wins with your team. You're ready to launch.

21

Launch Your Noble Purpose

It's time to engage your entire organization. This is where you put a stake in the ground that says, "We're doing something different. We're building on the best of who we are, and taking it to the next level."

Put Your Purpose in Front of Your Team

Whether your firm is small or large, you want to do an official launch. Whether it's a global summit, a Town Hall, or a product launch, it's psychologically important for you and your team that you do something public.

Your first inclination might be to kick off your launch by sharing your NSP. We've learned that a bit of context and framing up front will make your message more compelling, and thus more powerful. Here's the order that works best along with some talking points:

1. **Compelling customer-impact story**

   Open the meeting with the most compelling customer story that you have. Then say, in some version of your own words, "For me, this is our true purpose as an organization, to help customers like this citing the story. The team and I want to bring our purpose to life in an even bigger, bolder way."

2. **Three big discovery questions**

   Say, "We asked three questions." Share the three big discovery questions and the answers you gave in narrative form. Make sure you describe the team who worked on the process, so people know you had field input.

3. **Audience engagement**

   Ask the audience to answer the three big questions in pairs or small groups. Because you've done your homework, their answers will likely mirror the contents your team put forth.

4. **NSP reveal**

   After group discussion, poll them for their answers. Summarize, saying, "These are some of the same things the team and I recognized." Share another story. Then say, "We believe it's important to have a cohesive statement that describes our purpose as an organization." Now share your NSP. Explain why it's called an NSP and clarify who your real customers are.

5. **Personal backstory**

   Share what the NSP means to you; tell your team why you're all in. Let them know that you're launching this initiative to give their work more meaning and to add even more value for customers.

6. **Accelerators**

   Say, "When we looked across our organization, we saw opportunities to bring this to life immediately. Here's what's we're doing right now." Share your Accelerators.

   I've provided this level of detail because we know this works, and we want to make it easy for you. You don't have to reinvent the wheel. We've given you framework for your launch. Your job is to fill in the content. The following is the meeting flow.

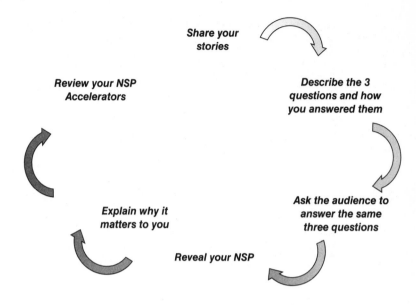

B. Internalize Your Purpose by Department

Figure 21.1   Purpose Launch Meeting Flow

Internalize Your Purpose by Department

Now that you've shared your NSP broadly, you want everyone in your organization to internalize it. You'll use the same three discovery questions you used when you created your NSP. Each manager should facilitate a session with her team, where they answer the three questions in the context of their department. It's important at this phase that when talking about the customers, that they do *not* turn the conversation towards internal customers. For example, your finance department should connect the dots between their daily activities and the people you have identified as customers. Your operations people should talk about how their work can be differentiated from the competition in the eyes of the customer.

Stop!

Are different departments working with NSPs? Make sure everyone is aligned with one NSP.

You did this as a leadership group, when you created your NSP. It's important that each department have the opportunities to have the same conversations. They are not tasked with changing the NSP. These discussions will help them internalize it. The act of discussing the three questions increases their level of engagement.

Each department should then create their own stories. The stories for marketing are different from the stories for manufacturing. The stories should directly pertain to the role their department plays in activating your NSP with customers.

You also want each person to articulate why the NSP matters to them, just as you articulated why it matters to you. Just as everyone wants to know the leader's backstory, everyone should also have their own backstory to increase their personal attachment.

To summarize, the process for department meetings is:

1. Answer the three discovery questions.
2. Create stories that substantiate the NSP.
3. Describe why the NSP matters to you.

In the most successful organizations, every single member of the company can:

Your NSP is what you do.

Customer-impact stories describe how you do it.

Your personal backstory articulates why it matters to you.

Create the Sharing System

To ensure that your NSP does not die after your big sexy launch, you need to quickly (within 30 days) create an ongoing sharing system. It might be a *Sell It Forward* weekly memo like Blackbaud or a quarterly *Beyond the Numbers* update like Hootsuite.

You want to create a simple system to ensure that every member of your organization regularly hears customer-impact stories. In some organizations, the leaders send a 25-word email each morning; other organizations have a monthly Town Hall that they open with a customer story. Look at what you're already doing and how you can incorporate customer-impact stories.

Deal with Cynics and Setbacks

You're compelling and on-point. You've moved hearts and minds. You have a concrete implementation plan that shows you're serious. If we lived in a perfect world, that would be enough. In reality, there are two kinds of challenges you'll likely face.

Enthusiasts

Your marketing team gets so excited that they want to make it the centerpiece of their new campaign. Your HR team says, "This is a training initiative," or "This fits perfectly with our culture program." Your social responsibility team can't wait to launch it as an outreach initiative. Be careful. Noble Purpose is all of these things, but if you let it become *one* of these things, you'll lose its power. At its core, Noble Purpose is a commercial model. It is a business strategy to help you win in the marketplace, and with your team. Invite your marketing, HR, and social responsibility teams to support the process. Build on their enthusiasm by giving them specific tasks to bring this to life within their roles. You want to harness their enthusiasm, but you don't want to let Noble Purpose sit inside one department alone. Do not let this become departmentalized or you risk it becoming marginalized.

Naysayers

The cynics are out there. You might have some people who either:

Don't believe this.

Don't want to be a part of it.

If this represents less than 10 percent of your people, don't waste your time on them. Your consistency will prove to the cynics that you are serious, and those who truly don't want to be a part of a purpose-driven organization will eventually self-select out. This is a good thing.

Stop!

If your cynic is a critical leader, don't try to use logic to convince them, create a scenario that enables them to experience your Noble Purpose.

22

Operationalize Your Noble Purpose

This is where you operationalize your Noble Purpose. That means bringing it to life in daily operations and using it as a framework for decision-making.

Find Your Noble Knights

Stop!

Your Noble Knights might not always be the most outspoken. Keep an ear out for muttered phrases like "I always thought this way."

During your launch phase, your exemplars likely emerged. These are the people who were living your Noble Purpose before you named it. They're high performers who want this to be successful. These are your Noble Knights.

This should be a cross-section of people who are recognized leaders and are embedded in critical areas of your operation. You may have a champion in each country, or each department. They don't all have to be at the same level. This may be a growth opportunity for a high-potential newcomer. Another member may be a senior leader with a strong track record of getting things done. You want people who are engaged and can make things happen.

Within 60 days of your launch, choose your team and pull them together. This group will be tasked with operationalizing your purpose at every level of the organization. They'll look for creative ways to bring your purpose to life, and concrete ways to measure your purpose. This is likely to include refining your key performance indicators (KPIs). They'll be looking across the organization to identify what you're already doing well, which you can leverage, and areas where you may be out of alignment with your purpose.

The Noble Knights should be empowered to make recommendations and be confident that they will have the resources to implement them. This group should also be charged with identifying the training required for the balance of the organization to implement your purpose. The Noble Knights are the team who will implement the following strategies.

Bring Customers to Life Throughout the Company

You want every single person in your organization to have a personal understanding of who your customers are and what their daily lives look like. Keep customers alive in their hearts and minds by bringing customer imagery into your physical spaces, and giving your team the opportunity to spend time in the customers' world.

For example:

- Use photographs of actual customers with their quotes on the walls of your customer service department.
- Include real customers in product development meetings.
- Have operations people spend a day in the life on site with customers.

- Codify customer personas including psychographics and backstory motivations and share broadly.
- Create screensavers with your NSP along with customer photos and stories.
- Create a mindfulness practice to help people become fully present with customers.
- Leave an empty chair representing the customer in every meeting.

Every department should have visual representations of your customer front and center.

Choose Your KPIs

Now that you've gotten a sense of what Noble Purpose looks like in action for your organization, you'll want to look at your KPIs to identify how you can enhance your metrics. These will be specific to your industry. It might be things like customer performance, client retention, customer comments, and so on.

Stop!

You don't want to make your system of measurement more complicated. If anything, you want to make it simpler.

You don't want to make your system of measurement more complex. If anything, you want to reduce the number of things you measure. Hone in on the most important performance metrics that will tell you whether or not you are living your NSP.

Declare Your Purpose Externally

At last, this is what your marketing department has been waiting for. Once you've solidified your purpose inside the company, it's time for you to share it externally. Be careful—declaring your purpose publicly is about more than slapping your NSP on your website. Sharing your NSP externally means clearly demonstrating to existing and potential customers the impact that you can have on their lives and businesses.

Ways you can do that are:

- Customer-impact testimonials. What it's not: customers simply saying how wonderful you are. What it is: customers describing the impact your products and service had on them.
- Teach customer-facing people how to incorporate compelling customer-impact stories into their interactions.
- Reframe your pitch deck so that it begins with a placeholder for your customers' purpose and mission. Set an expectation that presentations kick off with customers' goals. Then describe how your purpose is a commitment to helping them accomplish their objectives.
- Include your purpose in user training. Design the training that helps users to experience the impact described in your NSP.
- Train your service and delivery people to ask deeper questions about how your products are impacting customers.

Make the Tough Calls

Your team is aligned around your purpose. You've brought it to life inside and outside your organization. Now it's time to make some decisions about your future. It's likely that during the first three phases your team identified places where you are out of alignment with your purpose. Now is the time to address them.

What habits do you need to kick? Don't be discouraged if your stop-doing list has more items on it than your start-doing list. Give yourself space to say no, and don't be afraid to go first.

You also want to identify things that you are doing well that you want to leverage. These are the things that you are going to become known for.

Use the 6-P model as a framework to guide you (see Figure 22.1).

Your decisions at this phase will determine the strategic future of your business. You might decide to give up a product line or

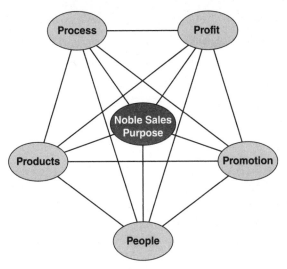

Figure 22.1

go into a new market. You may even decide to make structure or personnel changes.

If you are facing a challenging decision on your stop-doing list, ask your team, "What could we do instead that would improve life for our customers and put us in better alignment with our purpose?"

Make a Fuss, Routinely

Make sure you incorporate an element of celebration into your daily operations. The celebration needs to be pure. It's celebration about the positive impact you have on customers. There's no *yes, but . . .* to dampen the message. In addition to infusing celebration into daily operations, also consider stand-alone celebrations at the end of a quarter or year, where you can bring in customers and celebrate the totality of the impact you've had: how many people you've touched, how many lives were changed, how many businesses were improved, and so on. Celebrating the impact you have on customers demonstrates to your team that this is why our company exists.

23

Embed Your Noble Purpose

This is where you create the systems and processes to ensure that your purpose becomes part of your organizational DNA. Your purpose should be so integrated that it no longer requires a team of champions, it has become the essence of who you are as an organization. Many organizations never get to this phase. Those who do create organizations that transcend their industries.

Hire and Recruit with Purpose

When you become a Noble Purpose company, you attract candidates who are drawn to your purpose. The most successful companies devote an entire interview to test for culture fit. This is how you determine whether the candidate is a purposeful person, and whether he is aligned with your purpose. You want to create a screening process that identifies candidates who are excited to be part of your purpose, and use their skills to activate it. Look at organizations like HubSpot who post their Culture Code on SlideShare. They do a separate interview just for culture, as does G Adventures and Hootsuite.

Your executive search teams should be even more intentional about using purpose as a screening tool. Executives who are not aligned with your purpose can have a chilling effect on your entire organization.

Evaluate with Purpose

Your purpose should be present in employee assessments and job descriptions. Whether it is a qualitative measure like "Googliness" or a quantitative measure like customer satisfaction, all employees should be clear that they are expected to embody your purpose and make progress towards it within the scope of their jobs. You want to include the essence of culture fit and direct job performance.

Bring Your Board on Board

To ensure that your purpose lives on beyond senior management changes, your board should make your purpose part of their charter. It is their responsibility to evaluate the organization's performance against your purpose. This ensures that senior leaders do not get caught up in short-term thinking for the sake of quarterly earnings. Your board acts as the safeguard to keep the organization pointed towards what matters most.

Spotlight in Your Annual Report

You should also include your purpose and your progress against your purpose in your annual report. Your shareholders and stakeholders will come to expect that you will regularly report on your purpose progress. They will understand that your purpose drives competitive differentiation, and long-term market value.

Closing Thoughts

Never doubt that your work matters.
A tribe of True Believers who are driven by a Noble Purpose
do more than create a great organization.
They demonstrate to the rest of the world what's possible.
Making money and making a difference are not incompatible.
This duality is the birthright of every person on this planet.

Acknowledgments

It is with deep gratitude that I thank the people who helped bring this book, and these ideas into fruition:

First and foremost, my creative partner Elizabeth McLeod, whose ideas and experiences made this book better, and whose editing, writing, and graphics skills enabled team McLeod to finish strong.

Our clients, whose early Noble Purpose initiatives and willingness to share their stories made these concepts stronger and more applicable: Blackbaud, Commonwealth Assisted Living, Explorys, Foundation Supportworks, Flight Centre, G Adventures, getAbstract, Google, Graham-White, Hootsuite, Kaiser Permanente, MMS, Porter Keadle Moore, Pharmedium, Roche, Seneca Medical, ShelfGenie, and Thompson Dehydrating.

The experts and leaders, whose interviews and comments helped bring this to life: Cheryl Bachelder, Donna Brighton, Adam Grant, Brian Halligan, David Lapin, Bob Patrick, Melissa Reiff, and Raj Sisodia.

The "Super Friends" mastermind group, whose expertise and support show up in many obvious, and some not so obvious ways: Robbie Kellman Baxter, Scott Edinger, Seth Kahan, Libby Wagner, and Scott Wintrip.

My mentors, consulting expert Alan Weiss and positioning guru Mark Levy, who have guided all of my business endeavors.

The teams at Conscious Capitalism, Forbes.com, and TEDx for giving me platforms to share my ideas.

The team at John Wiley & Sons, who have been supportive publishing and promoting partners, on this and other endeavors.

My family, the fabulous Bob McLeod, Alex McLeod, and Elizabeth McLeod (second mention purely personal), who remind me that the only real end game is love.

Index